COUNTY LIBRARY

D1093837

*Painting the Human Figure*

TWO NUDES *Courtesy, ACA Gallery, New York.*

MOSES SOYER

# *Painting the Human Figure*

*Edited by Robert W. Gill*

WATSON-GUPTILL PUBLICATIONS *New York*

*Library of Congress Catalog Card Number: 64-24247*

*Edited by Donald Holden*
*Designed by Betty Binns*
*Composed in Eleven Point Baskerville by Western Printing and Lithographing Company*

*To Ida*

ACKNOWLEDGMENTS

*I wish to thank Don Holden, Editor of Watson-Guptill Publications, and Robert Gill for their kindness and patience; artist John Koch for his good words; and Sidney Bergen, who cajoled me into this enterprise.*

# CONTENTS

# INTRODUCTION

A FEW DAYS AGO, I had occasion to reread a treatise on the art and technique of the fifteenth century Flemish masters. What a sense of discipline, and—curiously—what a source of excitement and inspiration I found in this work! How infrequently may the serious student *really* know the true thought of a great artist! Modern teachers, especially the most sensitive and personal, often cannot impart their most considered and important thought; modern teaching, with its over-size classrooms, its "star" teachers (rarely themselves of equal importance as artists), renders serious, personal communication difficult indeed.

What joy it is to find the deepest, the sincerest, the most deliberated thought of a great contemporary artist awaiting us all! This is something one has had small hope for.

A grateful number of the nineteenth century painters (Delacroix and Ingres, for example) have written realistically and, hence, eloquently of their own procedures. We are all very much in their debt.

Never has there been a greater flow of words, more obfuscating pseudo-esthetic verbiage than during the last fifteen years, a great deal of this, I regret to say, by painters themselves. And yet, so little writing of their personal revelations, of their procedures, convictions, the things which long experience and dedication alone can give; the simple things which have sustained inspiration. I say *simple,* yet how subtle and mysterious they are!

As I read the pages of Moses Soyer's *Painting the Human Figure,* I see with what a warm and generous hand he has given of all of his deepest experience. How could it be otherwise in an artist so warm and so generous?

The words evoke the paintings. As I read his initial paragraphs on drawing, I see his *own* drawing, drawing on paper, drawing in paint. How illuminating, how undidactic, and how exact his instruction is! Who else has spoken with this evocative simplicity of the power of older painters to open contemporary horizons? Whether he discusses Eakins or Rubens, Monet or Ruisdael, suddenly I see the exact truth of the reference. I have been awakened to technical awareness charged with potentiality for *any* serious artist, whatever his years or experience.

I have time and again regretted that almost no truly serious and engaged modern painter has elected to write openly and without reserve about those innumerable aspects of art, of experience in art, of life predicated on art.

Here: it has been done. It will give enormously to the young who will read it avidly, the many young who have almost lost hope of finding such a work. And it will have great significance for all of Moses Soyer's generation as well.

*John Koch*

*Painting the Human Figure*

# 1 THE NUDE IN ART

A BOOK devoted to the figure should consider briefly the history and significance of the nude, particularly the female nude, since the female figure is fundamental to painting.

From the beginning of art, the nude has epitomized man's ideal of beauty. It has been depicted in many ways because nothing is so changeable as the human concept of beauty. Using the nude thematically and symbolically, the artist has expressed hope, despair, sin, religious fervor, ecstasy, and other basic human emotions. In modern times, the artist has painted the female nude in the most intimate moments of behavior, unobserved by others, unidealized and unadorned; he has expressed a mode of life. A study of the artistic interpretation of the nude throughout history unfolds a fascinating story of man's yearnings for a seemingly unattainable goal: ideal beauty.

Art is older than history. Years ago, I read a touching story of a cave girl who, moved one day by a strange impulse, seized a piece of charcoal from the burning hearth and traced the shadow of her lover on the wall of the cave. Was she the first artist to depict the human figure?

If we wished to be thorough, we should begin with the earliest known representation of the nude, the prehistoric "Venus of Willendorf." But



YOUNG GIRL *Collection, Mrs. Fell Douglass.*

this would not, I feel, serve the purpose of this book, which is primarily about how to draw and paint the human figure.

## *Classical and medieval art*

Let us, then, begin with the Greeks and end with Degas. In their interpretation of the nude, male and female, the Greeks perhaps came closest to attaining the human concept of ideal beauty. In pursuit of perfection, they invented their own anatomical measurements. They created their gods in the image of man and they made man god-like. They transformed the faceless, gross goddess of fertility into a radiant Venus. More than any other art in history, Greek art nearly reached perfection in creating an ideal man and woman.

This concept was lost and the ideal of beauty forgotten with the beginning of Christian art in the fourth century. For nearly a thousand years, the idea of original sin colored and influenced European art. The human body became a symbol of shame and sin; nakedness became associated with the devil and the damned. And the artist, who was the pictorial historian and the interpreter of his time, changed the glorious, faultless Venus into a stark, forbidding, almost dehumanized Eve. He covered her with heavy draperies which all but hid her body, because the body was the "gateway to hell."

## *Flemish primitives*

It took centuries for the nude to emerge again, tentatively at first, almost stealthily, until early in the fifteenth century, when the Van Eyck brothers painted their wonderful Adam and Eve in the Ghent Altarpiece. Roger Van der Weyden, Hugo Van der Goes, Hans Memling, and other Flemish masters slowly began to disrobe their men and women.

Memling painted his "Bathsheba in her Bath," which is simply a representation of a life-size nude woman, graceful, somewhat Gothic in appearance, emerging from her bath, while an attendant is enveloping her in a white towel. It is a lovely painting. There is hardly any religious significance to it, unlike the figure paintings of the Middle Ages. It is simply an excuse for painting the nude.

INTIMACY *Here is an interior with two young women—one semi-nude and the other clothed in a blue-green robe. The legs of the reclining figure are draped in brilliant yellow fabric. The background, bed, and floor are painted in blues and grays. Courtesy, ACA Gallery, New York.*

## *The Renaissance*

With the Renaissance, the age of humanism, came recovery of freedom for the human spirit, after the long, oppressive bondage of the Middle Ages. With freedom came a desire for knowledge: a desire to fathom the mysteries of life, to learn about man, to rediscover oneself. Science, philosophy, art, and poetry flourished; man regained his self-esteem and dignity.

It was an age of archeological discoveries; the beautiful Greek gods and goddesses filled the Renaissance artist with admiration and wonder. He based his art on the classical art of the Greeks. Man became proud and unashamed once again. The naked body of man and woman, as with the Greeks, became the central theme in Renaissance art.

The freedom and the opulence of the Renaissance are well expressed in the full bodied, rich female nudes of Giorgione and Titian, and the muscular, turbulent male figures of Michelangelo and Tintoretto. Truly, the art of the Renaissance, like that of the Greeks, was a glorious hymn to the beauty of the human body.

## *Rubens and Rembrandt*

After the Renaissance, which let light into the world, came the Baroque period. Its greatest exponents were Rubens and Rembrandt, two utterly dissimilar artists in whose work the nude plays a major part.

Rubens' male and female figures are robust, earthy, full-bodied, and lifelike. Rubens was completely physical and unspiritual. He painted the Virgin Mary, the Magdalene, and Christ himself in the same manner, and with the same attitude, as he did Diana, Hercules, and Jupiter.

I visited Rubens' lovely Italianate house in Antwerp. In his garden

INTERIOR WITH TWO FIGURES *In this picture of two figures in a room lit from above, the foreground figure, partly in shadow, is removing a white slip. The screen behind her is hung with blue and white drapes. The couch is blue, the wall and floor warm grays. Collection, Mr. and Mrs. Elliot Robinson.*

stood the statue of the burly Greek Hercules, which was the model not only for Rubens' Jupiter, but for his Christ as well. His male figures are bronzed, muscular, and aggressive. His females are soft, white, and yielding. His art is religious, yet pagan. He was one of the most masculine artists in history.

Rembrandt was the first great modern. He painted three important female nudes. The earliest is Danae. It represents a woman (his first wife, Saskia) in bed completely nude. He shows her in bed with an eager, inviting expression on her face, and an outstretched arm as in a gesture of welcome. She awaits her lover, Zeus, king of the gods. It is perhaps the most intimate portrait of a nude woman in art. Yet, paradoxically, it is imbued with spirituality.

Then he did a small painting of his second wife, Hendrickje, called "A Woman Bathing." This painting is completely modern in concept, a work either Courbet or Degas could have done. It represents a young woman raising her chemise above her rather knobby knees, wading in the water. The gesture of the figure is awkwardly touching and human. This painting foreshadows Courbet, Manet, and Degas, and even twentieth century paintings.

In his later years, he painted "Bathsheba in her Bath" (Hendrickje again). It is one of the most profound and spiritual paintings of a female nude in the whole history of art: a near life-size painting of a woman, not old, but whose body shows that she has experienced sorrow and has mothered children. Rembrandt painted her with great love and psychological insight. He placed her against a dark, luminous background, without decorative accessories or embellishments. She is lost in thought and the viewer is not aware of her nakedness.

## *The nude in Spain*

Reacting to the strict religious spirit of the country, the Spanish masters seldom painted the nude, especially avoiding the female figure. Velásquez painted only one nude—a Venus—one of the loveliest, slender, modern nudes in the world. El Greco's elongated, undulating nudes are completely asexual and spiritual. They could be angels without wings. Goya's modern, sloe-eyed "Nude Maja" is the direct forerunner of Manet's "Olympia."

MARIE-LISE *This half-length figure is carefully placed off-center to create an effective balance of light and dark areas. Although this canvas is actually quite small, the bold strokes and textures give the painting a powerful sense of scale. Collection, Mrs. Ida Soyer.*

*Detail of figure at right.*

TWO WOMEN *In this painting, I used the same model in two different attitudes. The colors of the flesh harmonize with the umbers and the ochres of the background. I also painted the shadows in tones of brown. Notice the strong contrast of light and shade. Courtesy, ACA Gallery, New York.*

## *Nineteenth century French painting*

Like the human concept of beauty, the philosophy of art changes with the times. In the work of Courbet and Manet, the precursors of the impressionists, the artist's treatment of the human figure underwent a drastic change.

The age of industrialization and materialism seemed to have no need, no place, for gods or goddesses. The male nude went out of existence almost completely. The male model was used only in art schools, as he still is today, to study anatomy, movement, etc. The female nude, however, was painted with as much fervor as ever. But she, along with the times, underwent a complete transformation. She ceased to be a vehicle through which the artist strove to express ideal beauty. The artist painted her simply as a woman, realistically and physically, for his was a search for visual truth as he understood it. She became simply *woman,* no longer Venus or Eve.

Then came the wonderful impressionists, the discoverers of light: Renoir, Degas, Pissarro, Monet, and others. Of them, only Degas and Renoir need concern us here. Renoir, perhaps, was the only modern who tried to return to the Greek ideal of the female nude without, however, sacrificing the spirit of his time. His serene, joyous, full bodied women take you back to the perfect Greek maidens. They are more coarse perhaps, less ideally proportioned, but they are alive and in their way as beautiful.

Degas' influence on my own development as an artist is second only to the influence of Rembrandt. Degas was one of the greatest draftsmen of all time. He was, like Ingres, whom he so admired, a master of line and movement. His art is clear, sharp, straightforward, often pitilessly analytical. Renoir, on seeing a Degas drawing of a nude woman, observed: "It is as profound as the Sermon on the Mount."

Paul Valéry wrote: "Degas was trying to find in the (female) nude the unique system of lines which would formulate the given movement of a

NUDE WITH BLUE CLOTH *This painting is an example of chiaroscuro (the balance of light and shadow in a picture). The figure is largely in shadow with strong highlights on her cheek, shoulder, and knees. A heavy blue drape and gray brick wall make up the background. Collection, Mr. Fred Foreman.*

RECLINING NUDE *There are strong contrasts of light and dark in this painting of a sleeping figure half draped in brown. The floor and wall are also brown, and the sheets and pillow are white. There is a blue curtain on the wall. Collection, Mr. and Mrs. Philip Wise.*

*Detail of torso and drapery.*

BLONDE NUDE *This is a supine figure on a blue couch. The foreshortened model is brightly lit and very delicately modelled. I painted the picture very thinly, creating something of the quality of a watercolor or a pastel. Private collection.*

body with the greatest precision and greatest possible generality." He is a master of intimacy. He hated ostentation in art as well as in life. His art is so pure that it is almost abstract.

One day, when Degas was showing his pastels to the writer, George Moore, the artist said: "Nudes until now have always depicted people as we imagine them. But my women are simple, honest people. Look at this one; she's washing her feet. It's as if you were looking through a keyhole."

This is hardly a complete history of the nude in art. The artists I mention are simply those who have influenced me most in the painting of the figure. Study them and try to learn their secrets.

# 2 LEARNING TO DRAW THE FIGURE

THE *Encyclopaedia Britannica* defines drawing as the "Art of delineation or of portrayal by means of line." Drawing has also been called the handmaiden to the art of painting. In order to paint, it is necessary to to learn how to draw; drawing and painting are inseparable.

A good painting is judged not only by its painterly qualities—composition, color relationships, textural application—but also by its skeleton, the drawing underneath. How beautifully *drawn* are the swirling, complicated compositions of Rubens and Delacroix.

It is perhaps true that artists are "born"; but the ability to draw comes only through hard work and constant application. It is not easy to put on paper what one's eye sees and one's mind selects. Drawing requires discipline and diligence. Drawing demands great skill, which, as in any art form, is acquired by experience.

Ingres, one of the great draftsmen, says in his notes: "If I had a school of painting, I would inscribe a sign on my door saying, 'School for Drawing,' and I am certain that I would bring forth painters." He further states: "Drawing is everything; the rest is hue." How sadly different is this point of view from that held and practiced by the art educators of today.

YOUNG ARTIST AND MODEL *Collection, Mr. and Mrs. Murray W. Primoff.*

RECLINING NUDE AND NUDE COMBING HER HAIR *These two drawings were done in charcoal on a sheet of hand made watercolor paper, which lends a rich texture to both line and tone. The soft gray tones are simply smudged with the finger. Courtesy, ACA Gallery, New York.*

Drawing is the most intimate and revealing part of an artist's work. Nothing in the world is more beautiful than a drawing by Rembrandt. It is often simply an idea, a thought put down on a scrap of paper. Yet, it is a complete and perfect work of art in itself.

It is a great satisfaction and a joy to be able to draw well. An art student should make it a practice to draw daily. Carry a small sketchbook at all times. Draw the members of your family at home; draw friends; draw yourself in the mirror; sketch the children in the park; sketch in the subway. The only way you will learn how to draw is to *draw*. The only way to train the eye, the mind, and the hand to work in harmony and coordination is to draw. Drawing is discipline.

## *Materials*

Beginners often ask whether they should begin to draw with crayon, charcoal, pencil, or pen. It really does not matter very much, but I feel that charcoal is perhaps the best choice. Charcoal is soft and easier to correct than pencil.

Pen and ink is the most difficult medium for a beginner. It demands precision and accuracy.

As for paper, it is a mistake to draw on cheap paper such as newsprint, which tears easily and soon becomes dry and brittle. Good paper—like good linen canvas, good brushes, and good paints—helps the artist. You will find it more satisfying and easier to get textural quality on good paper. I suggest better quality charcoal paper or "all purpose" drawing paper, suitable for pencil, charcoal, and ink.

One should respect one's materials. A good artisan uses good tools.

## *Color in drawing*

The introduction of color into drawing, as in the case of Watteau, can be useful and effective. Using only charcoal, reddish crayon, and white chalk, Watteau achieves a richness in his drawings, a fullness of form and a feeling of light, greater than many of his contemporaries achieved in their most complicated paintings.

M. Soyer

## *Toned paper*

Later on, you should try drawing with charcoal on toned paper, gray on tan. Use some white chalk to express light or to accentuate form. Study the great charcoal drawings of Degas. A bit of white chalk, intelligently used, makes the drawing come to life.

A drawing by Gauguin stands out vividly in my memory. It was a preliminary study for the great "Ia Orana Maria" in the Metropolitan Museum of Art. The drawing was in red crayon, gone over partly with charcoal. Here and there, Gauguin very sparingly used white chalk. It is a beautiful drawing, monumental and serene.

## *Learning by drawing from casts*

I was taught to draw in the old way: that is, drawing from plaster casts. Today, a student usually begins with a live model. Perhaps it is better this way, more stimulating, warmer, and less mechanical. Yet there is something in this old-fashioned way of drawing from casts.

A story is told of Renoir who, when already quite well known, decided that he was not a good enough draftsman. So he began to draw from casts; he made hundreds of drawings during a period of several years. It is good discipline.

Cézanne, the revolutionary, drew from casts even in his mature period. He owned a sculpture of a cupid, the French sculptor Puget's "Milo of Crotona" and a figure of a flayed man. He drew from them constantly and often included them in his still life compositions.

I used to love certain plaster objects: the head of Michelangelo's slave, for instance. I would lay it down or lean it against a stack of books to study foreshortening. I would turn it a hundred and one ways and draw.

NUDE STUDY *This is a monochrome painting done entirely in shades of brown, a study for another picture of a dancer in the same pose, but dressed in leotards and an orange skirt. A preliminary study from the nude can be very helpful. Private collection.*

I also had a flawless Greek head of Venus of which I was very fond. I was sad when it fell from its precarious perch as I was drawing the lovely head. It broke into a thousand pieces. I enjoyed drawing from that cast.

## *The live model*

It is, of course, more interesting and more exciting to draw from a live model. In school, having drawn for two or three years from plaster casts and having won a "mention" for a very careful, academic study of a Greek torso, I remember that I was finally admitted to life class. I shall never quite forget the first night.

I must have been about sixteen or seventeen at the time. The room was crowded. The night was hot and the electric lights were glaring. I was all anticipation.

Suddenly, the model came out from behind the screen and took a pose on the modeling stand. She was plump and middle-aged, with heavy breasts. She was a revelation to me and at the same time a great disenchantment. She was blonde, and due to the heat, I suppose, she looked pink, almost vermilion. I had not seen a woman completely nude before and she seemed gross and ugly; not at all like the beautiful Greek maidens and goddesses I had drawn from plaster casts. I was confused and saddened by this first experience in a life class.

Today, of course, I would have loved to draw or paint that woman. She was not young, but she was *human* and her body, as I look back, was deeply expressive.

When I was young, my brothers and I posed for one another. We were acquainted with the drawings of Rembrandt and Michelangelo and we would draw one another in the poses drawn by these masters. It was an exciting and challenging way to learn.

SEATED NUDE, BACK VIEW *This is a study in sanguine, a reddish crayon popular with the old masters. The warm tone of this crayon allows the artist to render flesh with great richness and subtlety. Like charcoal, sanguine can be spread with a fingertip. Courtesy, ACA Gallery, New York.*

*Detail of head and torso.*

YOUNG WOMAN DRESSING *This half-draped figure of a young woman holding a white slip covering her loins is a richly textured and thickly painted picture. I used warm, silvery grays. The bent head is almost completely in shadow. Collection, Mr. Louis J. Martin.*

M Soyer

## *Learning by drawing from memory*

After having sketched from a model, go home and try re-drawing the sketches from memory. In this way, you acquire valuable memory training.

This is an important skill which the great Oriental artists learned so well. Art teachers in China and Japan take their students to the zoo and tell them to sit and observe a lion or a tiger. The students look at the animal for hours and then go home and draw it. This is a very good way to learn to draw from memory.

I am sad to say that my own visual memory is not the best, but I do insist that my students go home and make memory drawings and then bring them to me for criticism. They line up the two drawings—one from life, one from memory—and compare how well they remembered.

Daumier, for instance, drew and painted exclusively from memory. Perhaps that is why his drawings and paintings are so eloquent. There are no details; there is only the gesture, the expression, the movement.

## *Drawing from photographs*

Photographs can be useful in drawing, but the student must first learn to draw from three dimensional objects: casts and live models.

Thomas Eakins, who was a great experimenter in photography, made use of photographs in his work. Degas also used photographs. But the important thing is that they used photographs as a point of departure; they did not simply copy. What Degas observed in photography were the accidental effects in lighting. And he discovered a fresh view of composition.

A model who posed for the modern French artist, André Derain, told me that he would take many photographs of her, perhaps twenty or thirty before he would start a picture. He probably took the photographs just to

STUDY FOR PORTRAIT OF JULIA EVERGOOD *Watercolor, pen and ink, and touches of pastel were used in these studies for a portrait which is in the Whitney Museum. This illustration demonstrates my method of developing a picture. Collection, Museum of Modern Art, New York.*

M Soyer
1962
Studies for
a portrait of Julia Evergood

NUDE SEATED IN ARMCHAIR *An awkward pose, like this one, can often be as striking as a more conventional, graceful pose. Degas had a great ability to capture the beauty in awkward views of the figure. The medium is charcoal on hand made paper. Courtesy, ACA Gallery, New York.*

learn about the light or movement, for he then disregarded the photographs completely and painted the model.

### *Starting a drawing*

Most beginners do not know how to start a drawing. Some start with the eyes, some with the foot, and some with one line.

The way to start a drawing is to study the model for a long time, as much as ten or fifteen minutes, in order to grasp the movement. Then lightly draw a few preliminary or imaginary lines which, although they may not really exist, will give you the idea of the movement and the proportions. With these guiding lines, you can proceed, starting perhaps with the head. Keep in mind the proportions and movement as you draw freely, broadly, and completely without details. When you have the whole thing, then you can work over some of the details and correct the mistakes. But you must have the whole conception in your mind as you draw.

Do not leave out toes, fingers, and ears. Remember what Michelangelo said: "Trifles are details, but details are not trifles."

When doing a portrait or a figure composition, I always make a number of drawings first. The first week, I simply draw the model in all kinds of poses and movements. I get to know the model in this way and this knowledge helps when I begin to draw on canvas. By then, I know the characteristics of the model and proportion and expression are easier to capture.

### *Shading*

When one talks about line and shading, one must clarify the meaning of the word *form,* which is much used in conversation about art, but little understood. It is through line and shading that an artist defines form. By the word *form,* the artist means shape, the weight or volume of shapes, or the arrangement of parts.

Line does not exist in nature. Line is an invention, a symbol. Line, however, is a means of expression by which the artist describes the shapes of nature.

Shading, as well as line, is an invention, a means of expression. Shading helps to render form, volume, modeling, and the weight of things. Through shading, one expresses light.

The Japanese artists use line superbly. The line drawings of Matisse and the early drawings of Picasso are exquisite and will teach you a great deal about the use of line. One should strive in drawing for an economy of means, for a line which is direct and expressive.

Leonardo da Vinci, Michelangelo, Raphael, and Degas, on the other hand, combined line and shading. Their drawings are profound. In the drawings of these great artists, shading always expresses form. The student should bear in mind that shading for the sake of shading means nothing; it merely becomes an academic formula.

## *Copying the masters*

When I was young, I was offered a summer job as a political cartoonist on a newspaper, while the regular cartoonist was on vacation. I was completely inexperienced and fearful, but I had two books of drawings, one by Rembrandt and the other by Daumier. I kept these books in my desk. All the characters I needed—all the movements, all the gestures—were in those two slim volumes.

If I had to draw an arrogant politician accused of misdemeanors, there was the wonderful self-portrait of Rembrandt in studio attire, self-assured, hands on hips, looking you straight in the eye. Or if I had to draw a group of strikers demanding better working conditions, there were the insurrectionists by Daumier. All my models were in these books. All I had to do was change the attire and the mood; but the gesture, the movement was there.

Was this unethical? I do not think so. I was young, I needed the job desperately, and I had a great deal to learn. Those books were my teachers. How grateful I am that I could learn from Rembrandt and Daumier.

DANCERS *Here is a group of four female nudes painted in monochrome—browns and tans. The seated figure in the foreground contrasts with the standing figures to form a dynamic composition, and the overlapping forms produce imagined depth. Collection, Mr. and Mrs. Philip Rosenberg.*

Students should not only draw from life or memory. They should also copy the drawings of the great masters, and make drawings from the paintings of the masters. But you should *not* copy blindly, exactly and without emotion, but copy freely, imaginatively. Do not complete your copies. Stop when you feel that you have gotten what you set out to learn.

Try to grasp the flow of line in a nude drawing by Ingres. Discover the sense of movement in a prancing horse by Delacroix. Copy Raphael, Michelangelo, and Degas. Study the sfumato—the gradual transitions of tone from light to dark—in the drawings and paintings of Leonardo.

A drawing by Rembrandt is more difficult to copy than a drawing by Michelangelo because Rembrandt's line is intangible and spiritual. His drawings seem to be dictated by his spirit rather than drawn by hand. They are deep and penetrating and full of color.

Artists learn from one another. Goya copied Velásquez; Degas copied early Italian masters; Delacroix and Cézanne copied Rubens; Fragonard copied Rembrandt. There are two Crucifixions hanging side by side in the Royal Museum of Brussels. One is by Rubens and the other a copy of the Rubens by Delacroix. They are the same, yet how different! How "pure Delacroix" is the copy.

Fragonard copied Rembrandt's Madonna rocking the cradle, part of the great "Holy Family" in the Hermitage Museum of Leningrad. Fragonard transformed the deeply human Mother into a pretty, charming French girl, a "pure Fragonard."

Do not copy slavishly; rather, try to understand and to learn.

I cannot overemphasize the importance of studying the great masters, old and modern. Study their work in the museums. Great paintings are to the art student what great novels are to the student of writing.

STANDING NUDE, LEANING ON HER KNEE *This is a typical quick study, made before I began to paint. I encourage the model to take a variety of spontaneous, relaxed poses, and I continue drawing until I find the pose I prefer to paint. Courtesy, ACA Gallery, New York.*

# 3 THE MODEL

A MODEL need not necessarily be a professional. I seldom paint professional models. To me, non-professionals are far more interesting and stimulating, even though they may not always sit as quietly as a model should.

## *Selecting the model*

The people I paint are often art students, dancers, members of my family, fellow artists, friends—people I know well, or get to know in the process of painting—people whose facial features and body characteristics I find interesting. You should not experience too much difficulty in persuading friends and fellow students to pose for you if you are willing to reciprocate, because art students are gregarious by nature and like to work in groups. I treasure many memories of the Saturday and Sunday afternoons of my art student days when a group of us, idealistic boys and girls, not satisfied with the school routine, would get together in someone's smoke-filled attic and pose for one another. We'd criticize each other's drawings—cruelly but honestly—and endlessly debate the problems that were facing us. We dis-

BLONDE NUDE *Collection, Mr. and Mrs. Joseph Kahn.*

M Soyer

cussed the relative importance of Piero della Francesca and Cézanne; the meaning of form and volume; composition and space relationship; as well as the problem of how to live and study at the same time (we were all very poor). Often we talked well into the night about life, love, and immortality. We had a glorious time and we learned a great deal from one another.

You will find that young people with lean, lithe bodies are of great value in learning about anatomy. Their muscles are taut and firm, not hidden by fatty layers, nor sagging like those of middle-aged or old people. Dancers, workmen, prizefighters and the like make very good models. Accustomed to bodily movement, they can take poses arranged in sequence, thus demonstrating how the body works in action: how dependent one part is upon another; how the forward thrust of the neck or the leg affects and influences all other parts of the body. Everything works in unison and harmony, no matter how slight or violent the movement.

When I said that young bodies are more suitable if you wish to study anatomy, I did not mean that an art student should confine himself to one type of model. Nature is so extravagantly rich, she never repeats herself. There are no two leaves on a tree that are exactly alike; each human being is a world unto himself, both spiritually and physically. Each human being has two eyes and one nose; yet how vastly different they are from one another. The artist's task is to explore these differences, to delve deeply into the character of his model and try to fathom the mysteries of nature. The great paintings of the world are not always inspired by the young and the beautiful. The women of Rembrandt are even homely, perhaps, but how profoundly human they are, how familiar. Have you not met Hendrickje (Rembrandt's second wife) one day strolling down the street? I have. Nor could the immortal Mona Lisa of Leonardo da Vinci be called pretty by our present day standards. An old woman upon whom life has left its scars, whose hands are gnarled from hard work, is as good a subject for the artist as the most beautiful young woman.

SEATED DANCER *This picture represents the model sitting in a rather stiff attitude that only a dancer could take. She is dressed in a black leotard and orange skirt, and is leaning against a brilliant blue wall. Note the strong verticals, horizontals, and diagonals. Collection, Ida Soyer.*

ROOMMATES *Here is a large painting of a nude and semi-nude girl seated on a bed with blue cover. The background figure wears a blue skirt with purple flowers. The wall is painted in blues and grays, and a chair draped with yellow cloth is at the far left. Collection, Mr. and Mrs. Melvin Haft.*

"You must bear in mind," said John Sloan, the famous American artist and teacher, "that the model is a human being . . . that it is alive. Look at the model with respect. Appreciate his or her humanity. Be very humble before that human being. Be filled with wonder."

## *Paint your own face and figure*

One of my favorite models—most patient and willing—is myself. I am neither young nor handsome, but in a mirror and in the solitude of my studio, I can study myself, full face and three-quarter view. With the aid of another mirror, I can see myself in profile. I can study facial expressions, proportions, moods, movements. I can study hands, and if the mirror is large enough, I can study my whole body either nude or clothed. One thinks of Leonardo da Vinci and how wise he was when he said: "The mirror, above all, the mirror is our teacher."

It is not an exaggeration, I think, when I say that most figurative artists have at one time or another drawn or painted themselves. An artist paints himself not because he is vain or because of self-love, but because he sincerely wants to know himself more fully, to probe more deeply into human psychology. By learning about oneself, one also learns about others.

Rembrandt left about seventy self-portraits: drawings, etchings, and paintings. They constitute a profound and moving autobiography of a genius. Study and emulate him. Study the works of the masters. You can learn a great deal from them. When Cézanne was asked who his teacher was, he replied caustically: "The Louvre."

## *Costume, makeup, hairdo*

Generally, I prefer to paint the model in his or her natural state, in everyday clothes. If a girl comes to my studio with lips shaped to emulate some famous movie star, her eyes painted to resemble the latest conception of Cleopatra, and with a B. B. hairdo, I say, gently so as not to hurt her feelings: "I should like to paint you without makeup, pretty though it is. I would like to paint you perhaps the way you look in the morning, when you are alone and unobserved, before you go out. Bring your old sweaters and bandannas." If the girl should have long hair, I may ask her to fix it in a somewhat untidy bun, which is always pleasant to paint.

I remember seeing a watercolor by Cézanne. It portrayed a heavy, old jacket flung carelessly over a chair. The jacket had individuality and character. It was shaped, through long wearing, by Cézanne's body. It was almost a portrait of Cézanne—intimate and touching—and it told me about the great artist's loneliness, and his habits, more than a thousand words could have said.

In painting the clothed person, one must bear in mind the body inside the clothes. I advise my students to make a number of preliminary nude studies of the model before attempting to paint. Clothes should not conceal the body, but rather reveal it. Clothes should express the character and acquire the form of their wearer, like Cézanne's jacket.

Do you recall the lovely "Madonna of the Chair" by Raphael in the Pitti Palace in Florence? She is a young, beautiful girl "of the people," with a round face and full, graceful body. She tenderly holds the Christ Child in her arms. She is dressed in the voluminous clothing of the Renaissance. One would think that the body would vanish completely inside these heavy velvets and brocades. Yet the contrary is true. Observe how the clothes caress and cling to the Madonna's body; how much a part of her they are; how physically revealing they are. One could almost make a drawing of her nude body from this painting (Cézanne's jacket all over again).

Yes, one can learn a great deal by first painting and drawing the figure nude, then clothed.

## *Choosing the pose*

Before I begin to paint, I usually talk to the model, to get acquainted and to put him or her at ease. We continue conversing while I work and, in this way, I learn a great deal. The expression changes and the model's charac-

SELF-PORTRAIT *This is one of many self-portraits I have painted in recent years. I was not satisfied with this picture and put it aside for several months. Then I completely repainted it, suppressing details and using a palette knife and brush. Collection, Mr. and Mrs. Louis Friedenthal.*

teristics reveal themselves, more than if the model just sat or stood motionless and silent.

I have the model take a standing or sitting pose, or a reclining pose, and I do a number of quick studies in pencil or charcoal. In this way, I learn the bodily peculiarities of the model. After a while, you will notice that the model falls into poses that are natural, not strained, trite, or academic. When a certain pose strikes me and I see possibilities for a painting, I ask the model to hold it and I make more drawings.

This time, the drawings are more careful, more complete "studies in the round," rather than linear impressions. I try to coordinate line, form, and movement. I begin to model, to strive for solidity and texture. In other words, I begin to formulate and express my thoughts and feelings visually. I distort, elongate, and try to get at the essence of things. I say to myself: good drawings are not necessarily the correct or the academic drawings. The drawings of El Greco are not judged by the proportions of his figures. The drawings of Rembrandt, Ingres, Van Gogh are eloquent, emotional, and profoundly expressive, never merely correct. Correctness alone will never make a drawing great.

The more studies you make, the more deeply you familiarize yourself with your model, the more profound your final painting will be. Some artists claim that the first impression is the true one. It may be so, but a good work of art, in my opinion, is the result of many impressions, many states of mind. Surely Leonardo's "Mona Lisa" is not the result of a first impression.

It is said that Rodin, the great French sculptor, had a number of nude models walk around in his studio, pausing to sit or stand as they wished. When a pose interested him, he would make a rapid sketch in pencil and watercolor wash. These sketches were, it is true, first impressions, evocative and lovely. On occasion, these quick drawings become ideas for future works. But his Balzac required years of research and more than forty studies

JOAN *This is a study of one of my favorite models. She wears a blue and white striped robe and is painted against a gray wall. This model also posed for "Young Nude," which is reproduced in color in this book. Collection, Ida Soyer.*

DANCER IN A BLUE SKIRT *Black leotard, blue skirt, and gray wall form a long vertical picture that is carefully drawn and painted. The hands and figure are in a dance attitude. It is a somewhat earlier work. Collection, Mr. and Mrs. Charles Renthal.*

*Detail of head, torso, and arms.*

—some complete and wonderful in themselves—before the final work was completed.

In an art school *life class,* one has little choice of model or pose. There, the nude model is in a given attitude viewed from whatever angle you are obliged to take, because of your place in the classroom. However, having chosen your spot, I would advise you to observe your model from all angles. Walk around the model. Study how the same pose looks from the back and the side. This will help you to understand the pose more fully, whatever view you finally draw.

## *Good poses for the beginner*

The least complicated pose to draw or paint—and the best pose for the beginner—is a standing figure viewed from the front. Then, try the same pose from the side and the back. After that, vary the pose, changing the movement, but not too drastically. Change the position of the arms, for instance, or a leg. You will find that the smallest movement of a limb or a muscle affects every other limb or muscle of the body.

The same applies to a seated figure or a reclining figure. First try a simple pose from the front, then from the side and from the back. Later you may vary the poses as you wish.

## *Relating the figure to the picture format*

As a beginner, if you are going to paint a reclining figure, you will do well to use the canvas horizontally. For a standing figure, you will probably want to place the canvas vertically. However, there are many different things one

MARILYN *This painting of a young girl seated on a couch, leaning on one hand, is painted very sketchily—almost as if it were a drawing in paint. It is in blues, purples, and grays, with warm flesh tones. The paint is quite thin. Courtesy, ACA Gallery, New York.*

can do. For instance, when I am painting a very tall young man and I want to emphasize this tallness, I use the canvas vertically, even though he may be seated.

In composing a picture, it is not necessarily desirable to place the figure in the center of the canvas. Sometimes a figure placed all the way to the left, or to the far right, enchances the composition and gives the picture a feeling of the unexpected. In photography, one can see the exciting possibilities of placing the figure off center or even allowing the figure to be cut by the edge of the canvas.

The old masters, it is true, composed their pictures in a very careful, systematic manner, and not spontaneously. They were like architects building from blueprints. But the modern artist sometimes gives his pictures the informal, accidental quality of a snapshot. Degas, Bonnard, Vuillard, and others composed many of their works in this manner. Of course, this is not to suggest that careful planning of your picture is unnecessary or passé. Try working both ways.

## *Relating the figure to background and surroundings*

The background is a very important part of figure painting, and I feel that it is not stressed enough in art schools. You are taught how to paint the figure in a vacuum, without concerning yourself with the rest of the canvas. You are told about proportion and color, perhaps, and then you are left to "fill in" the background. Painted in this way, the figure does not live, does not breathe, and it appears pasted onto the canvas. However, if you consider the background and surrounding area as part of the picture while you paint the figure—if you attempt to harmonize the whole—the figure will become part of the fabric of the picture, not merely an isolated fragment in your painting.

GYPSY *I painted this girl with black hair and black eyes in a black dress set against a deep red background. A green drape is over the chair. The light face and hands contrast sharply with the darks of the rest of the picture. It is thickly painted. Courtesy, ACA Gallery, New York.*

In addition, a great deal of character is revealed if one paints the figure in those surroundings which are indigenous to that figure. Personally, I like to paint simple people, dressed in simple, everyday clothes, and I put them in a milieu of simple everyday objects. Whether the model is nude, half nude, or fully clothed, it is good to paint her in a setting which is natural to her and which explains who she is.

As for props, a table, a chair, pictures on the wall, something that is in harmony with the figure—in form, color, and character—can add much to your painting. An object or objects placed behind the figure can be useful in suggesting a feeling of depth. Let us say that I paint a woman sitting at a table in a room, and I want to express a feeling of considerable distance between the figure and the background wall. I place a bed or chair behind the model, or even show another room in the distance, and thereby enhance the illusion of three-dimensional depth in my picture.

## *Group compositions*

In painting a group of figures, one must arrange the poses to fit the composition.

In my pictures of dancers, for instance, I have often used one girl for all the figures. If the dancers appear similar in size, this similarity will make the picture more harmonious. In a picture of this type, one should not try to render the model's features or physical type too exactly. One should rather use the model symbolically: use her *general* form. Degas followed this procedure. I am sure that El Greco, in some of his huge compositions, used one model for all the figures.

Also in my compositions of dancers and other figure groupings, I try to give the impression that there is no central story in the painting, no central direction. Each girl is a world unto herself. One walks one way; one

FELIX *Though this figure is seated, I painted him on a long, vertical canvas in order to accentuate his long, thin body. Using several blues, with touches of tan and white, I freely drew and painted, emphasizing the boy's angularity. Courtesy, ACA Gallery, New York.*

walks another way; one kneels. What unites them in the picture is the overall movement or gesture, and the distribution of color. This makes my pictures of dancers somewhat more abstract; abstraction and distortion are inherent in all art. The worst, the most dreadful thing in art would be an absolute copy of nature: figures painted without imagination, without an idea, without distortion.

If, however, one wishes to express a central idea in which all the figures participate as one—as in my painting, "Apprehension," which groups men, women, and children in an attitude of fear—then the figures must be united psychologically and compositionally. Good examples of this are seen in Daumier's dramatic paintings of insurrection.

## *What to paint*

Renoir, on being informed that Gauguin went to Tahiti to paint, shrugged and said: "One can paint in Batignolles as well."

On leaving school, young artists are often frustrated and baffled when they must decide on their subject matter. What should one paint when everything seems to have been painted already? The answer is simply that *everything* is good to paint. One does not have to go to an exotic country for material. It is all around you.

While Gauguin was rediscovering himself in Tahiti, his great contemporaries were painting the life around them. Degas in Paris, Cézanne in Aix, Renoir in Batignolles—they all painted a small world which they loved and knew intimately. The fact that their predecessors painted the same things did not worry them; they knew that the important thing in art is not so much *what* you paint, but rather *how* you look at things, and *how* you put your interpretation on canvas.

If you have eyes that see, plus an inquiring and probing mind, then the block in which you live could be your Batignolles. You can find in it all the subject matter you could wish for, all the comedy and tragedy of life.

Rembrandt and the great American painter, Thomas Eakins, exemplify what I mean. Rembrandt lived and worked practically all his life in Amsterdam. He painted Amsterdam burghers and their wives, as well as the city's philosophers, doctors, and beggars. His model for Christ was a young Jew from the Amsterdam ghetto. Rembrandt painted the people around him with great depth, insight, and spirituality. Eakins, America's greatest artist, lived and painted all his life in his native Philadelphia. Like Rembrandt, he painted the people of his town—teachers, doctors, athletes—honestly and without compromise.

Each, in his own way, painted the people and the life he saw around him, as well as the landscape he knew so well. Both great artists transcended their locality and imbued their work with universal meaning.

# 4 MATERIALS AND METHODS

MATERIALS and equipment are certainly not the key to successful painting, but it is wise to choose them carefully and buy the best you can afford. A good brush, for example, generally costs more than a brush which is merely "acceptable." But the good brush will outperform —and probably outlast—the mediocre substitute.

Ultimately, you will develop your own preferences for specific colors, kinds of brushes and painting knives, canvas or panel materials. In this chapter, I will recommend a simple list of materials and equipment which you will find useful in the early stages of figure painting. As your work develops, you may continue to find this list sufficient—as I have—or you will begin to build a list of your own.

## *Palette*

I use a conventional, oval-shaped wooden palette for oil painting. It responds nicely to the brush and feels comfortable in the hand. It is a large palette and actually I never hold it, but keep it on a stand or table when



SEATED NUDE *Collection, Mrs. Ida Soyer.*

I am working. The choice of the oval shape is just a personal thing. Many painters prefer a rectangular palette.

A palette has to be kept clean. After you have wiped it off many times, the wood becomes quite beautiful and the surface is very pleasant to work on.

Some people like white paper throw-away palettes, but I do not care for them. They do not respond to the touch and I feel that paper presents an unpleasant surface for mixing.

Glass palettes are also used by many painters. Glass is easy to keep clean, but again, I think the surface is very cold and unsympathetic to work on. However, all these things are personal. In time you will develop your own preference for certain materials.

### *Brushes*

Bristle brushes are available with long or short bristles. I use long-haired bristle brushes as they are more pliable and I feel that they last longer. Advocates of short-haired bristle brushes point out that short bristles carry a heavier load of paint and produce more pronounced textures on the paint surface.

I also use some pointed sable brushes. They are easy to draw with and are almost like a sharpened pencil or crayon. One can also draw with the side of a flat bristle brush. Flat sable brushes will also give you a light, crisp stroke.

It is not absolutely necessary, but I like to have a considerable variety of brushes to choose from. Again, your own choice of brushes will depend upon how your personal painting methods evolve. I would advise the beginner to try brushes of all shapes and sizes, using the brush that seems right for the given task.

### *Palette knives*

There are two basic kinds of palette knives: those for mixing colors and scraping the palette; and those that are used to paint with.

A painting knife, either trowel-like or spatula-shaped, is very useful

CROUCHING NUDE *This is a rough and thickly painted picture in soft blues, light ochres, and deep warm shadows. I completely disregarded detail and concentrated on the large forms. The lights are thick, the darks transparent. Collection, Mr. and Mrs. Alfred W. Kleinbaum.*

for laying in large areas of color; for achieving certain textural effects; and for applying the paint very thickly. When you apply the paint with a palette knife, the color can be purer and cleaner than when you apply color with a brush. I like to use both brush and knife in a picture.

I think that when Rembrandt painted the light on a forehead, the reflections on jewelry, or strong light on drapery, he used a palette knife. In Goya's painting, "The Forge," in the Frick Collection, you can actually see the big slashes of the palette knife. These knife passages are wonderfully handled and give life and strength to the painting.

Some artists have used only the palette knife in certain pictures. Courbet was one of the great palette knife painters. Vlaminck was another.

## *Colors*

I use comparatively few colors. Artists have remarked about this. I feel that a few colors are adequate. I can express what I want with these colors.

In arranging colors on my palette, I start with white. Next come the yellows: cadmium yellow, light; at times, Naples yellow for a soft yellow; yellow ochre, of course. Now come reds and browns: cadmium red, light; raw umber; burnt sienna; burnt umber; and alizarin crimson. Then come the blues: cobalt, ultramarine, and sometimes cerulean. Last are viridian green, green earth, and black. Usually, I use ivory black; but if I want a matte quality in my painting, I use lamp black.

I use white lead—usually called flake white or Cremnitz white—mixed with Permalba white. This mixture does not yellow like zinc white or lead white alone; and the mixture does not crack as some other whites do.

You can mix violet, of course, but sometimes I use cobalt violet for its special brilliance.

GIRL IN BLUE *Here is a study of a nude draped in blue. The composition of the limbs and the broad execution makes this a strong, dynamic picture. It is painted thickly, using a background of blues and purples. This picture has the quality of a quick sketch in oil. Private collection.*

M Soyer

THREE WOMEN *While the central figure here is fully developed, the two figures in the background are merely sketched in. I painted the picture rather thickly with brush and palette knife. Notice the importance of the hands. Collection, Dr. and Mrs. Irving Wallach.*

*Detail of hands.*

The palette of colors that *you* use will eventually become a matter of personal choice. You will use certain colors that some other artists do not use. Matisse, for instance, used some very striking harmonies of strange colors; his palette was quite different from yours or mine.

## *Mediums*

A medium is the vehicle you mix with tube colors to produce the quality and consistency you prefer for brushwork. I use a very simple medium: linseed oil and turpentine, combined half-and-half. After having tried many mediums, I find this the most satisfactory.

Sometimes I mix retouching varnish with the oil-turpentine mixture to make the paint dry faster. Also, when the painting is dry and you want to work over it, spray or lightly brush on some retouching varnish to give the surface a somewhat tacky quality that allows the new paint to adhere well. The varnish will also prevent the fresh paint from looking like an obviously retouched patch.

I find that stand oil is a useful addition to your medium if you want to paint very thickly (with a heavy *impasto*). Rubens was supposed to have used stand oil and Venice turpentine in his medium. This produced an enamel-like quality when dry.

But for the beginner, I think it is important not to experiment too much with the chemistry of paint. It is important to apply oneself to *drawing* and *painting,* without too much experimentation. Use the simplest mediums and the fewest colors. Try not to get involved too much with other things. After a few years, when you have mastered drawing and painting, you can experiment. What is important is not *how* you do things, but *what* you do. Ultimately, you will acquire a language of your own, your own way of painting.

PORTRAIT OF JACK LEVINE *I worked on this portrait a long time, but tried to keep the appearance of a large sketch (except for the head). The paint is thinly washed on in most parts, and the head is thickly painted with palette knife and brush. Courtesy, ACA Gallery, New York.*

## *Canvas*

If you have the time, it is good to learn how to prepare your own canvas. The more you know about the materials you use, the better. Linen canvas is the best.

The traditional method is to tack raw linen on a frame made of wooden stretcher strips (bought in your local art supply store); wet the canvas slightly so it contracts, tightens, and becomes smooth as it dries; size the raw canvas with rabbit skin glue; and finally apply one or two coats of white lead, pressing the paint well into the fibers with a broad-bladed knife.

My own canvas is prepared by a somewhat more complex process, which I will describe as a matter of interest, but which you are unlikely to try until your own painting is quite advanced. As with all my materials, I use good quality canvas. It is prepared for me by hand, by Anjac Products. The following is a description of the process, given to me by Mr. Jacob Siegel, the chemist of the concern.

(1) Singeing: After stretching raw Belgian linen evenly on pins on the wood frame, the surface of the cloth is carefully singed to remove excess fibers sticking upwards. This is done so that moisture will not be absorbed by these tubular fibers.

(2) Sizing: The canvas receives two applications of French rabbit skin glue, containing an anti-fungi and anti-bacterial agent, introduced to prevent deterioration of the fabric. This preparation fills in the pores of the linen and becomes a base for the priming.

FOUR DANCERS IN ORANGE *In this study, the figures are in unrelated attitudes, dressed in orange and black. I painted it very freely and rather thickly, using a palette knife in the light parts. The division of wall and floor is left unmarked. Courtesy, ACA Gallery, New York.*

(3) Priming: The final gesso formulation, applied twice to the sized surface, comprises the following ingredients, plus water:

Titanium dioxide: this is a permanent white pigment.

Clay: a pure white earth ingredient adds body to the gesso composition.

Rabbit skin glue: this functions as a binder.

Acrylic: a pure, safe, synthetic resin gives flexibility.

Anti-fungi and anti-bacterial agent: this safeguards the primer.

In the past, the student of painting was apprenticed to a master and worked in his studio. The apprentice was taught how to grind colors, how to prepare canvas and gesso panels, and how to transfer drawings to canvas. He worked with the master all day and learning these basic crafts was the apprentice's only concern.

But we do not live in a Renaissance society and many students must work at other jobs while studying art. I had to work when I was a student and could not give up my whole day to painting as I would like to have done. I had to do as much painting as I could in the time I had. Fortunately, today we have many manfactured materials: paint in tubes; prepared varnishes and mediums; and prepared canvas. Everything is done for us. So if you do not have the time to prepare your own, it is permissible to use a good grade of prepared linen canvas. Prepared cotton canvas is sold, but I do not think it is a suitable support for oil painting.

### *Burlap*

Burlap is pleasant to paint on, but it rots and a painting done on it does not last long without professional restoration. I had experience with burlap when I was young. This fabric was very inexpensive and I liked the rough

MARY ANN *This dancer is not in her dancing pose. I drew rather carefully but I did not paint too many details. Brown hair, white slip, and delicate skin tones are set against a brown background. Private collection.*

Soyer

*Detail of head and hands.*

GIRL IN PINK *This young girl leaning on a table is wearing a pink blouse and I painted the background in greens and browns. I roughly suggested another head behind the girl. It is broadly executed in a somewhat expressionist manner. Collection, Dr. and Mrs. Arthur Barth.*

texture. But lately, one of those early painting of mine was brought to me by its owner. The burlap had deteriorated considerably; it was very brittle and had to be relined (mounted on new canvas) to be preserved.

Gauguin painted many of his Tahitian pictures on burlap. The great painting in the Boston Museum of Fine Arts, "Where do we come from? What are we? Where are we going?" is painted on burlap sacks sewn together. This rough material and the vigorous application of paint give this large painting a feeling of strength and solidity.

## *Canvas board*

Canvas board is all right for the student to start with. It is less expensive than canvas and you do not have the bother of stretching or preparing it. Naturally, it is best to use linen canvas board instead of cotton, but linen panels are more expensive.

## *Wood panels*

Wood offers a beautiful surface to paint on. A good oak panel is excellent, but you can use almost any kind of wood, properly seasoned. I have used wood panels prepared with gesso, or wood panels just varnished to seal the pores. A gesso surface is preferable; this glowing white ground preserves the brilliance of the colors.

The old masters used wood panels almost exclusively for their small pictures. That beautiful "Madonna of the Chair" by Raphael was supposedly painted on the wooden top of a wine barrel.

A popular and dependable modern panel material is Masonite, a composition of wood fibers, available in 4 × 8 sheets at any lumber yard. Be

SELF-PORTRAIT *I painted this small, three-quarter portrait thickly, using brush and palette knife. The colors are tans and yellows and strong opaque off-whites. The head is against the light, placing most of it in shadow. Collection, Dr. and Mrs. Arthur Barth.*

sure to get the kind labeled *untempered* and have it cut to the size you wish. The simplest way to prepare Masonite is with one or two coats of white lead.

## *Paper*

Paper has been much used for oil painting, from the early Italian masters to Holbein and Degas. George Bellows' famous picture, "Introducing Mr. Sullivan," was painted on paper.

Painting on paper, you get a certain quality that you do not get on canvas or wood. Paper has a beautiful matte effect. Use any good quality, heavy rag paper and prepare it with glue size or a light shellac. You can also use a gelatin solution. Or you can paint on the unprepared paper; but this is a little more difficult, because the paper is very absorbent at first and it takes longer to cover the surface. Furthermore, unsized paper soaks up oil and may deteriorate eventually.

## *Varnishing the finished painting*

I do not varnish my pictures with a final varnish. I use a retouching varnish as a final varnish. This is a very light varnish—available in spray cans or bottles—which freshens the final color.

Oil paint dries very slowly. A painting may be dry to the touch, but underneath the paint may still be wet, especially if you paint thickly. I feel it takes two or three years for a painting to really dry. This is the right time to use a final varnish, which is much heavier than retouching varnish, adds gloss, and forms a protective layer over the paint.

TWO DANCERS *These two dancers are about to get up from the floor. They are dressed in black leotards and brown and green tights. The olive-green background harmonizes with the color of their tights. The angles made by the arms and legs are very striking. Private collection.*

# 5 COLOR

IT is desirable for a student to limit his palette and try to learn to paint with as few colors as possible. By using only the primary colors—red, yellow, and blue—and by adding black and white, you can theoretically obtain almost any color you wish.

In reality, however, it is impossible to mix these colors and get a vibrant cobalt violet, a deep viridian green, or a cobalt blue. You *can* mix greens and violets, of course, but you do not get the exact hues of cobalt, violet, viridian, or cobalt blue. There are many secondary and tertiary colors—greens, oranges, violets—on the market today. If the student (advised by his instructor) carefully chooses the colors which appeal to him, he should be able to obtain a good personal palette. As time goes on and as his knowledge of color develops, the student may drop some colors in preference to others. But at all times, the palette should be limited, almost frugal.

A student once showed me a painting he did with the primary colors only. It was an accomplishment. He was—perhaps justly—proud of it. But the picture was prosaic, lifeless, and muddy.

THE REIDS *Collection, Miss Eartha Kitt.*

## *Learning to mix colors*

It is important for a student to learn how to mix colors intelligently to avoid ending with a dull, muddy picture. When I enter a classroom at the beginning of the week, I see the fresh palettes neatly arranged with bright, intoxicating colors. I hope that the students will be so moved by these yellows, reds, and purples, that they will not utterly destroy these colors by the end of the week, in the process of copying the model or the still life in front of them.

I do not mean that color must always be intense. Compare Van Gogh and Degas.

When you look at a group of Van Gogh's paintings, the colors in themselves—the yellows, blues, and greens—have a terrific effect on the viewer. Van Gogh expressed his emotions with very bright—and at times garish—colors.

Perhaps it takes a greater artist to express all these emotions with subdued colors. Degas is a good example. He used a very restricted palette to achieve depth and richness. In an almost monochromatic (one color) painting, he expressed all the emotions that one might express with a much greater range of color.

You should mix colors carefully and thoughtfully. Each color has within it a rich range of depth, tone, and intensity. There are, for instance, many grays: cool grays, warm grays, deep grays, etc. You should experiment; through practice, you will learn how to obtain the desired gray.

In mixing, you should always use as few colors as possible. The student who mixes all his colors in a desperate, random effort to obtain what he wants, ends up with mud. This applies to the mixing of all colors, from gray to the brightest hue.

There is one lesson you can learn from the non-objective painters, the

YOUNG WOMAN IN YELLOW *This is a freely painted study of a full-bodied young woman with blonde hair. The cool background contrasts with the warm flesh tones and yellow drapery. I used a large brush and palette knife to paint this picture. Collection, Mr. and Mrs. Philip Sills.*

abstract expressionists of today. That is that pure color, applied on canvas emotionally or even intellectually, can stir deep emotions. I remember a young student of mine who, during a period of emotional breakdown, was given canvas and paints by her psychiatrist. At first, her paintings were black and brown. Later, as she was recovering, she added deep reds and purples. Her last paintings were done completely in yellows and oranges. By then, she was on her way to health. She told me how moved she was emotionally as she put pure yellow on canvas. It was as if she were recapturing the warmth of the sun. It made her warm inside and communicative again.

"Color," said Van Gogh, "can suggest some emotions of an ardent temperament." In a letter to his brother, Theo, he wrote: "In my picture of the 'Night Café' (in the Metropolitan Museum of Art) I have tried to show (through color) that the café is a place where one can ruin one's self, go mad, or commit a crime."

Think of the warm colors in Rembrandt's profoundly moving "Jewish Bride": the rich, yet subdued scarlet of the woman's skirt; the golden, olive color of the man's cloak; the warm, transparent background. These colors help to express envelopment and love, which is the theme of this masterpiece. The colors in this picture do more than arouse an immediate, sensuous response. Like the colors in Van Gogh's "Night Café," they assume a symbolic significance.

## *Color harmony*

One talks a great deal about harmony in painting: about congruity, proportionate arrangement of color, etc. But harmony is not always attained through colors which are felicitous and go well together. It is often achieved with colors which clash: with colors which are opposites. In other words, dissonance, discordance can sometimes become harmony. Good examples of this seeming paradox can be found in the work of Van Gogh, the French Fauves, and the German expressionists.

The colors in Rubens' paintings often seem to shriek, so violent are his yellows, blues, reds, and violets. Yet, viewed in their proper setting, his colors fall into place and harmonize with one another. He was, perhaps, the most accurate and knowledgeable colorist of them all.

When I was in Antwerp some years ago, I went to see his "Descent

REPOSE *This picture of a young girl leaning on a pink cushion in a red-orange sweater and flowered skirt is a freely painted study for a larger picture. No attempt is made to delineate the chair, cushion, or background. Collection, Mr. Maurice Herman.*

from the Cross" in the cathedral. The painting stood on the floor in the process of being restored and cleaned. I studied the picture closely and carefully at eye level. It was enormous. The figures were larger than life. The colors seemed to be garish and brutal. The painting upset me. A year later, I went to see it again. The painting was hung in its place, high on the cathedral wall. The colors were majestic, sonorous, and beautifully orchestrated.

I love Corot's Italian landscapes and his portraits of girls. His work is firm and solid, yet quiet. His colors never clash. They are almost muted. There is an underlying brownish gray tone. Sometimes, in one of his silvery pictures, a blue or red kerchief on a girl's head or neck gives all the life and contrast needed in the picture.

You do not have to use all the colors of the spectrum to obtain a quality of richness and depth. The late work of Renoir is rich, lush and harmonious, with a unifying red undertone. His colors give you a feeling of the earth and of the growth of living things. He achieved this with very few colors. He would often paint a figure entirely in brownish reds, using white and Naples yellow for light and then paint a red drapery in the back of it.

Not being of a scientific nature, I have not investigated the various theories of color at any great length. I feel that an artist is guided by his inner spirit; in time, he evolves his own palette and his own theories of a personal, particular nature, a palette which answers his needs, and suits his temperament.

Art does not progress as science progresses. Great works of art were created before artists learned about proportions, foreshortening, perspective, or the science of theories of color. The prehistoric murals on the walls of the Lascaux caves are as expressive and touching as anything done in art since. And the compositions of Giotto are as deeply moving as those of Rembrandt and Courbet.

RAPHAEL SOYER *This is a portrait of my twin brother—a sketch rather than a finished painting. In a harmony of blues and grays, I tried to capture my brother's rather tense thoughtfulness. Collection, Mr. Sidney Lawrence.*

There is something mysterious about color. One can teach drawing and composition, but not color. One is not born with a "sense of drawing." But one *is* born with a "sense of color."

## *Grisaille*

Grisaille means monochromatic painting: that is, painting in various shades of gray. However, one can paint monochromatically in any color.

The old masters—the Van Eycks, Memling, Gerhard David, etc.—often painted sections of their altarpieces in grisaille.

Modern artists, too, have painted in grisaille. Ingres, for instance, painted two identical reclining odalisques. One of them is in grisaille; it hangs in our own Metropolitan Museum. The other one, in many colors, is in the Louvre. They are both complete and equally beautiful.

Géricault made a number of monochromatic studies for his "Raft of the Medusa." Some of Daumier's paintings could be called monochromatic. His "Don Quixote," in the Courtauld Collection in London, is painted completely in browns, as is his touching composition of Christ being mocked by the populace. Degas, Vuillard, and others painted monochromatically at times.

Nothing is more *colorful* than a little drawing done with a reed pen and wash by Rembrandt, expressing all the depth, distance, form, and gesture in just a little brown wash on white paper. Such a drawing has all the color that is necessary.

I too like to paint in monochrome. I feel free from worries about color relationships. Yet the process imposes a discipline of its own. Sometimes, after painting a figure in monochrome, I am tempted to add another color to the study. Perhaps I color the lips with a bit of pink or paint the slip white. But then, in the strict sense of the word, the painting ceases to be a grisaille or a monochromatic painting.

KEEN WALLACE *This is a friend of mine, a man who is a poet and translator. I painted his portrait in my studio, using purples, tans, grays, and yellows. The figure is placed well to the left of the canvas and the folding screen on the right acts to balance the composition. Courtesy, ACA Gallery, New York.*

YOUNG COUPLE *This is a painting of a young husband and his wife. She is dressed in a yellow blouse and blue skirt. He is wearing a blue shirt and brown trousers, and the couch is blue. The background is painted in various shades of warm gray. Private collection.*

*Detail of male figure.*

## *Local color*

For a student, it is necessary to begin by painting in local color: that is, the actual color of an object not influenced by reflected light. You must learn to paint a blue dress the proper shade of blue, brown hair the right shade of brown, and so on.

But remember that this is not the only way to handle color. When children start painting by themselves, they have no idea of local color. They just put the most brilliant colors next to one another, and sometimes, something very wonderful results.

However, the academies and the schools have taught us so-called local color. I do not know whether this academic concept is a blessing or not. But trained as I was in the earlier school, I believe in painting in local color. In fact, I believe that one can paint a picture as Degas often did, expressing all the colors virtually in browns, grays, and white.

The student should keep his mind open to many ways of handling color. But to begin with, he should learn to employ local color. Later, he can learn to deal with color more freely, more inventively, if local color does not satisfy him.

## *Chiaroscuro*

Chiaroscuro means the opposition of lights and darks, or the arrangement and balance of light and shadow in painting.

Caravaggio, Georges de la Tour, Zurbaran, and others used chiaroscuro effectively; but its greatest master, of course, was Rembrandt. One of his late paintings, "The Denial of St. Peter," is a fine example of chiaroscuro. The opposition of the lights and darks in this picture is caused by the lighted candle which a young woman holds in one hand, while shielding the candle with the other hand. The light of the candle illumines the head and body of the saint—making him the focal figure in the composition—and throws into the dark the armed soldiers who are in the foreground. The Christ group in the background, actually on the third plane in the picture, is dimly lit. This lighting (chiaroscuro) helps to create an extraordinary impression of a deeply moving drama.

The chiaroscuro of Rembrandt lacks the harsh contrast of light and

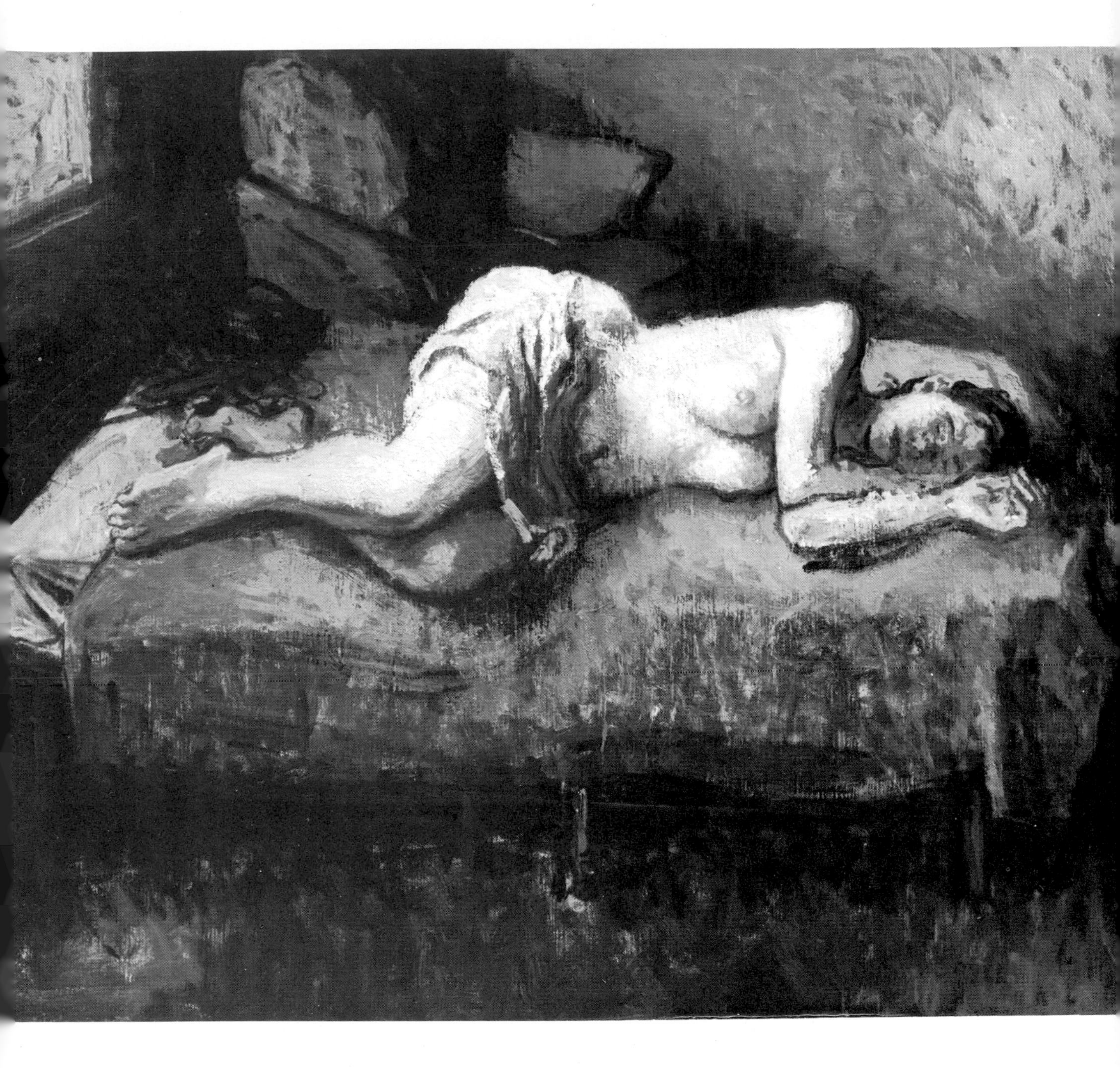

ASLEEP *This reclining nude, a white slip covering her hips, is lying on a blue bed. A green armchair is in the background. There are strong lights and shadows in this predominantly blue painting. Collection, Mr. and Mrs. Sidney Lawrence.*

shadow that we see in Caravaggio. Rembrandt's transitions are not as brutal; because of this, they are all the more spiritual.

## *Cool and warm colors*

Cool colors—like blue and green—recede. Warm colors—like red and yellow—advance. This can be studied in the work of the old masters—especially the landscapes—and of the impressionists as well.

Examine the landscapes of Patinir or Monet. You will find transparent blues and light purples (cool colors) in the distant hills and skies. As the planes advance toward you, the colors become warmer until the earth is all umbers and ochres, and you are almost within the landscape.

While the old masters had to rely more on perspective to achieve a feeling of distance, the impressionists were able to express distance through color alone.

## *Gray*

Gray is the support, the *binder* of all color harmony. All great artists have recognized the importance of gray and the greatest pictures contain a variety of grays. Even in his most brilliant paintings, Delacroix surrounded his bright colors with grays.

Because of these tonal grays, the reds and yellows an artist puts on his canvas seem stronger and more vibrant; more so than if all the colors were equally bright.

Bear in mind that grays are not mere mixtures of black and white paint. An infinite variety of warm and cool grays can be mixed from the most vivid colors on your palette.

ANDREA AND FELIX *The woman is dressed in a purple dress, long black stockings, and a blue sweater. The man wears a dark blue shirt and light blue trousers. I painted loosely and broadly and, although painted and re-painted, the painting retains its freshness. Courtesy, ACA Gallery, New York.*

## *Values*

Value means the gradation of tone from light to dark, or the darkness or lightness of a color. No matter how bright the colors are, it is important that they should not jump out of the picture. They should be in proper *value relationship*—in proper balance—with the other colors in the painting.

This is especially true in the richly colored work of a man like Bonnard, who understood color better than anyone else. Although he used the most intense oranges and reds, they never jump out of the canvas because the values are right. The value of each color is so related to the other colors that all the hues hold their places.

Every great artist—even artists like Kokoschka or Soutine, whose color is often violent—related his colors with very refined judgment. Colors are placed next to one another so that the most purple violet, the reddest red, and the bluest blue never jump out of the picture.

## *Flesh color*

As far as I am concerned, there is no such thing as "flesh color," even though tubes bearing that label are on the market today and are popular with art students. If you talk of "flesh color," whose flesh do you mean? A person of the white race? But when you paint a Negro or an Asian, the idea of "flesh color" becomes meaningless. In Picasso's "blue period" paintings, everything is blue, including the flesh; yet these paintings have more of the quality of human skin than do the portraits by academicians who use "flesh color."

The color of flesh is completely dominated by the light in which the model is posed, indoors or outdoors. We have learned from the impressionists that shadows can be completely transparent, even blue or purple.

STUDIO INTERIOR WITH FIGURE *This young girl in a green armchair is surrounded by a somewhat somber interior of blues, purples, and browns. There is a large, unfinished painting in the background and other canvases stacked about the room. Collection, Mr. Sidney Lawrence.*

NOEMI *The model, dressed in black with deep red sleeves, looks like a woman of the Renaissance. The background is painted in warm yellow-greens, and the whole is rather transparent because I used thin paint and glazes. Courtesy, ACA Gallery, New York.*



*Detail of head.*

One of the most sensitive colorists in modern art was Bonnard. In his interiors, the people are often anything but flesh colored. In one painting, for example, the bright yellow tablecloth throws an equally bright yellow into the face of the woman setting the table, thus creating a bright yellow flesh tone. The colors are completely in harmony and the figure looks human, alive, and quite natural.

Flesh takes on the color of its surroundings. If you are in a room with gray walls and all the things around you are gray, then the flesh really becomes gray, as in early paintings by Vuillard, in Corot, or in Giacometti. Certainly the deep brown shadows in portraits by Rembrandt are completely different from the shadows you see today, because we have more light in our homes.

## *Selecting the right color*

Suppose you are doing a painting of a group of dancers. The central figure wears a blue skirt. Somehow, the blue is not right, does not harmonize with the rest of the colors. How, then, do you select the right color?

One way is to make a small color sketch, substituting a different shade of blue, or even a different color, for the blue that does not satisfy you. If you feel pleased with the new effect, then cut a piece of tracing paper the size and shape of the skirt on the original; attach the tracing paper to the canvas with tape; and color the paper with pastel or watercolor in your newly selected color. Study it. If it still pleases you, remove the paper and proceed to color the skirt.

Matisse, in his old age, painted with colored papers only. He would cut out bits of colored paper and place them one next to the other. Although it was the work of an old and ill man, he achieved very unusual and beautiful harmonies.

GIRL IN STRIPED BLOUSE *Here I painted a pregnant young woman in a white and pink striped blouse. Her hair is blonde and she wears a blue skirt. The background is the partially covered toned canvas. The hands are expressive in their largeness. Courtesy, ACA Gallery, New York.*

## *Black and white*

You cannot paint without white. White gives each color a wide range; but you must be wary of mixing too much white with colors or they will become chalky, losing their strength and intensity.

As for black, it is one of my favorite colors. Black gives tone to color and thus gives harmony to the painting. Of course, the use of black has its dangers, too. If not used skillfully, black will make your colors dirty.

Talking about black brings to mind a remark by Renoir. He tried for years to mix a good black by using all sorts of colors, but he was never satisfied. One day, when he simply used pure black from the tube, he realized what a "noble color" it was.

Some artists, like Matisse and Rouault, have used black a great deal, mainly as an outline to emphasize form. This outline emphasizes the two-dimensional qualities of a painting.

## *Form*

Many modern artists paint in flat areas of color. Maurice Denis, the spokesman for the Nabis (followers of Gauguin), said: "A picture is a flat surface covered with colors arranged in a certain order." Matisse's paintings are flat. He completely discarded modeling in painting. His work fits into Denis' definition.

When I was young, the word *form* had a different connotation than it has today. One day, I said to Robert Henri: "Everybody talks about form, but what is form?" He replied: "Form is the weight and volume of things." As examples, he cited Rembrandt and Courbet. At that time, we thought

GIRL IN GREEN STOCKINGS *This seated, semi-nude figure in a white slip, purple skirt, and green stockings is quite thickly painted, especially in the flesh and light parts. The background is purple, and the hair brown. Courtesy, ACA Gallery, New York.*

this was a marvelous definition of form. However, if you accept that definition today, then you must conclude that Denis was wrong and that Matisse's paintings lack form completely, since they have neither weight nor volume.

Today, we mean something entirely different by the word *form*. Form is, first of all, the division of space. These divisions—these areas of space and color—are called form or *forms*. Thus, Matisse does not lack form. He *has* form in the sense of a flat canvas divided into areas of color.

## *Impressionism, Bonnard, and modern color*

What the impressionists did was to destroy the so-called local color. They opened up the windows, so to speak, and let in light and air. For them, light became diffused as it is in nature, as it is outdoors. A landscape by Monet is completely different from a landscape by Ruisdael, the greatest Dutch landscape painter. Monet painted the shadows in *color,* while Ruisdael (and the landscape painters before him) painted shadows in browns or grays.

To Bonnard, color became even more important than it was to the impressionists. He did not copy color as artists in the past copied light and shade, or the way the impressionists actually copied local color, to give us a sense of "the time of day." He intensified color. Color became important for its own sake. He exaggerated the purples, blues, or reds *beyond* what they are in actual light. His color intoxicates you.

Looking at a Bonnard, you almost forget the subject of the picture and look upon it as an abstract tapestry of the most beautiful colors. Bonnard stimulates an emotional reaction to a simple vase of flowers.

CELLA IN BLUE *This is a study very thickly painted in blues, tans, and grays with a palette knife and brush. As in most of my paintings, this one was completed without the model being present. Collection, Mr. and Mrs. Percy Uris.*

# 6 THE STANDING FIGURE

TO demonstrate how I paint a figure, I have first chosen the single, standing figure, seen from the front, with hands at the side, head slightly raised. This pose is basic to all figure painting, because it presents the figure in its most familiar attitude, with pelvis and rib cage in their basic alignment, and with a minimum of foreshortening. For the beginner, the standing figure presents fewer problems in drawing, proportion, and placement on the canvas. However, here the artist is obliged to interpret the figure in a simple, direct manner with an accuracy that does not allow for glossing over any of its elements. You must give equal attention to all parts of the figure, but in doing so do not forget the whole. Painting the single, standing figure is an excellent first exercise.

The standing pose will also show up defects in drawing, anatomy, and equilibrium.

This demonstration painting is simply a full standing figure, filling the canvas from top to bottom. The figure is centered, with no objects in the background. Instead, a semi-abstract spattering of color surrounds the figure.

AFTERNOON LIGHT *Courtesy, ACA Gallery, New York.*

## *First stage*

Before starting to paint, I made several sketches on paper to familiarize myself with the subject and to determine the composition.

Next, I chose a canvas of suitable size and shape and toned it with green earth. (Sometimes I use raw umber for toning but almost any neutral color can be used.) To thin the paint, I used a mixture of linseed oil and turpentine with a little retouching varnish to accelerate the drying. With a brush, I applied the paint, in a rather liquid consistency, and wiped off the excess with a rag. This kind of application leaves an even, transparent film of color on the canvas.

After toning, I allow the canvas to dry thoroughly, or paint on it while it is still tacky. I prefer to start the painting on a somewhat tacky surface because the paint adheres better, and the colors fuse more easily.

I then drew in the figure with burnt umber mixed with a little black and thinned with linseed oil and turpentine. Using a round bristle brush (the side of a flat bristle brush or a round sable brush will serve very well for drawing, too), I sketched the figure very roughly and freely on the canvas. Details such as facial features, fingers, and toes are merely indicated. I used a rag to wipe out any mistakes and then re-drew with the brush. Wiping out the paint leaves a brown tone on the canvas, and through the process of drawing and wiping out, one could almost complete an entire painting in monochrome.

## *Second stage*

In the next stage, I corrected the drawing: perhaps a shoulder was too wide or a leg extended too far. Working from dark to light, I laid in the dark

FIRST STAGE *I drew in the figure with burnt umber mixed with a little black and thinned with linseed oil and turpentine. With a round bristle brush, I roughly sketched the figure on the canvas. I freely indicated details such as facial features, fingers, and toes. I used a rag to wipe out any mistakes and then re-drew with the brush.*

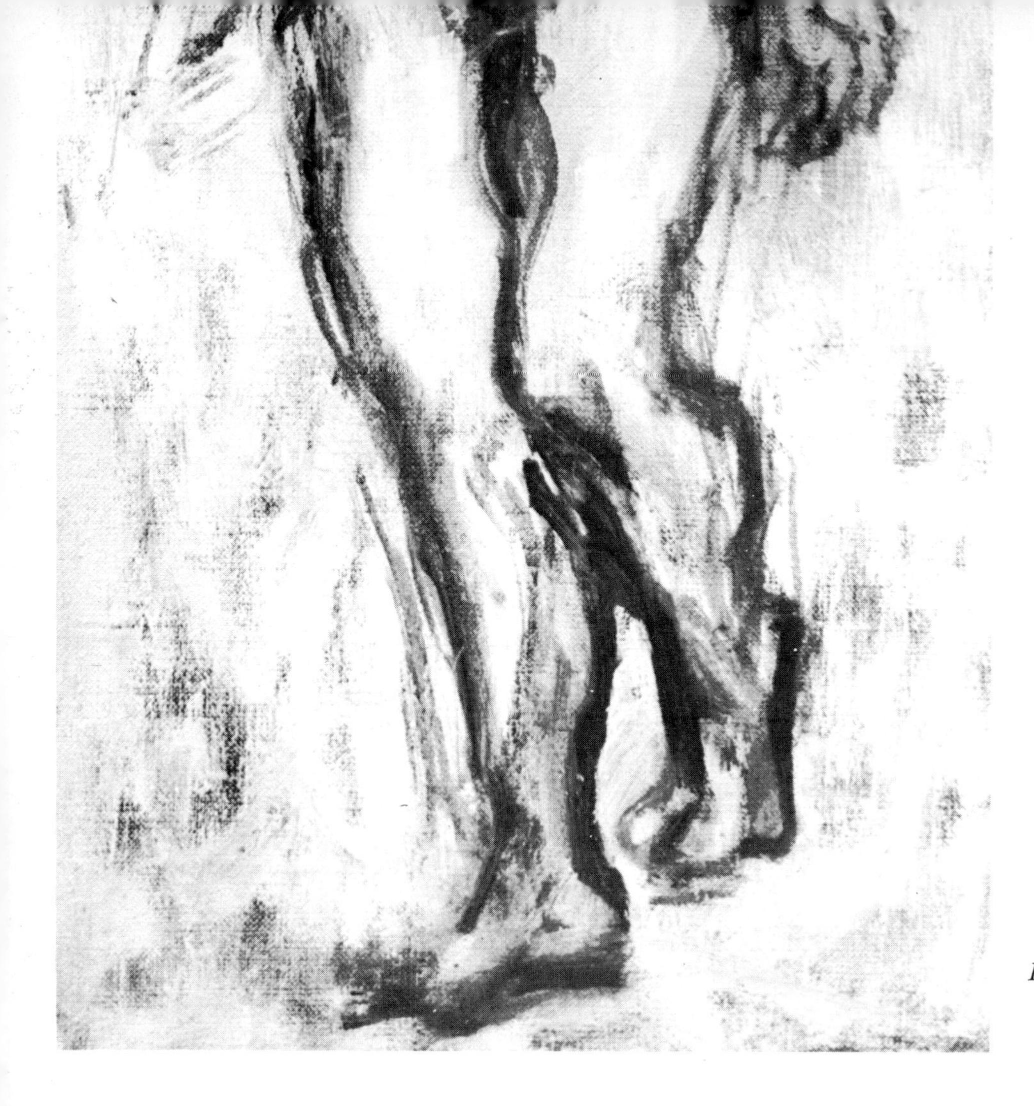

*Detail of legs, first stage.*

areas with burnt umber and slowly added the lighter areas, using a mixture of yellow ochre and white. As I painted, I continued to improve the drawing. Gradually the image grew—seemingly without effort, and the picture emerged through the process of painting.

Having decided upon the general color, I gradually laid in the different color areas. I painted an area, scraped off the paint, and re-painted. This scraping also adds to the painting surface, creating a kind of patina which gives texture and quality to the canvas.

SECOND STAGE *I first corrected the drawing. Working from dark to light, I laid in the dark areas with burnt umber and slowly added the lighter areas, using a mixture of yellow ochre and white. As I painted, I continued to improve the drawing.*

*Detail of torso, second stage.*

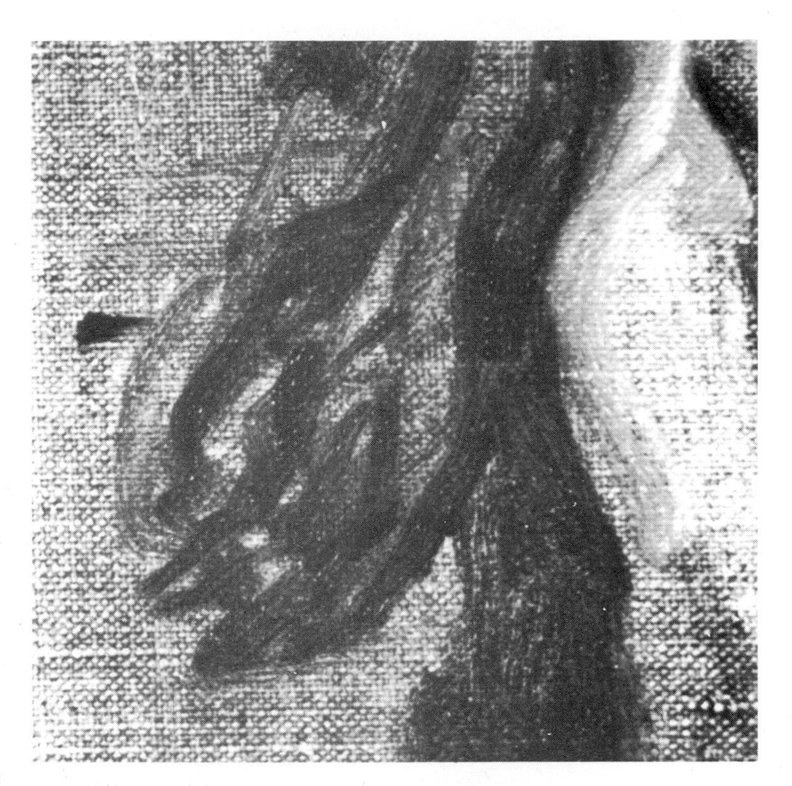

*Detail of hand, second stage.*

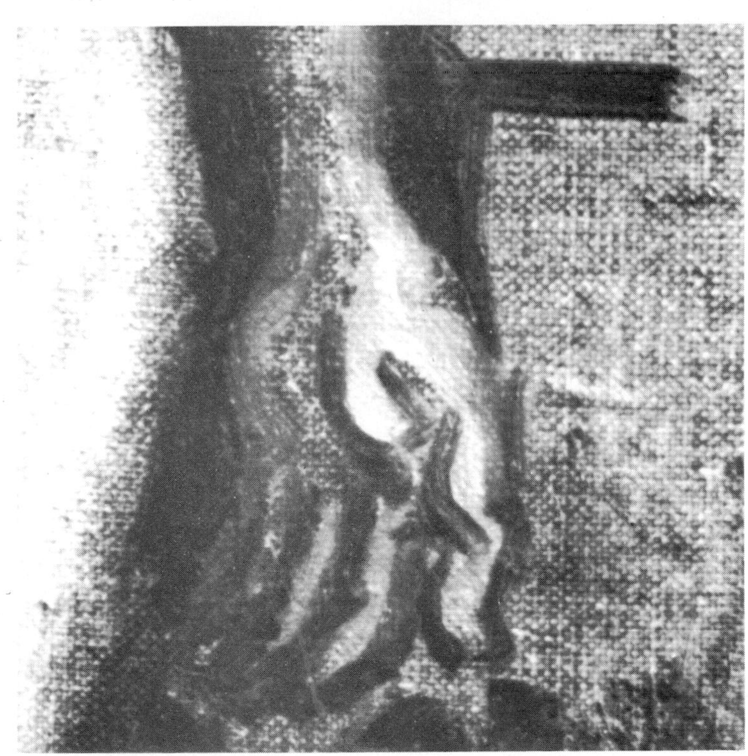

*Detail of hand, second stage.*

## *Third stage*

The third stage is the completion stage of the picture. I try to keep the dark areas and shadows transparent; I paint the light areas more thickly, sometimes using the palette knife to lay on the paint. Again I improve the drawing and work out the features, fingers, toes, and other details. The picture begins to take on the aspect of completeness.

It is important, however, not to over-finish a painting. It is good to leave some parts in a more sketchy state and other parts in a more finished state. Contrasting the degree of finish adds to the total effect just as it does when you contrast color and value. Where a seventeenth century Dutch still life painter, let us say, would aim for the most accurate rendering of an orange or a peach in his picture, the modern artist offers his *impression* of the piece of fruit, with a few broad brush strokes and a splash of color. Through his personal, excited handling of the paint, the modern artist almost allows us to participate in the process of painting.

The green to the right of the head, and the blue along the left side of the figure contrast with the warm flesh tones of yellow, orange, and red. I repeated the dark brown of the hair on the left side of the figure and at the base of the picture.

Having emphasized the importance of working directly from nature, I must add that I feel that the final stage of the painting should be done without the model. You should complete the painting alone in the studio. This is the time when you see the painting most clearly, most objectively. In these last few days or hours, you pull all the elements of the picture together, intensifying colors, muting colors, and above all, simplifying. Eliminating excess detail, simplifying a painting to its essentials, these are often the most difficult tasks of all. In these final hours, the artist's creativity and personality fully assert themselves.

THIRD STAGE *I try to keep the dark areas and shadows transparent, and I paint the light areas more thickly. The green to the right of the head, and the blue along the left side of the figure contrast with the warm flesh tones of yellow, orange, and red. I repeated the dark brown of the hair on the left side of the figure and at the base of the picture. The completed painting, titled "Standing Nude," is reproduced by courtesy of the ACA Gallery.*

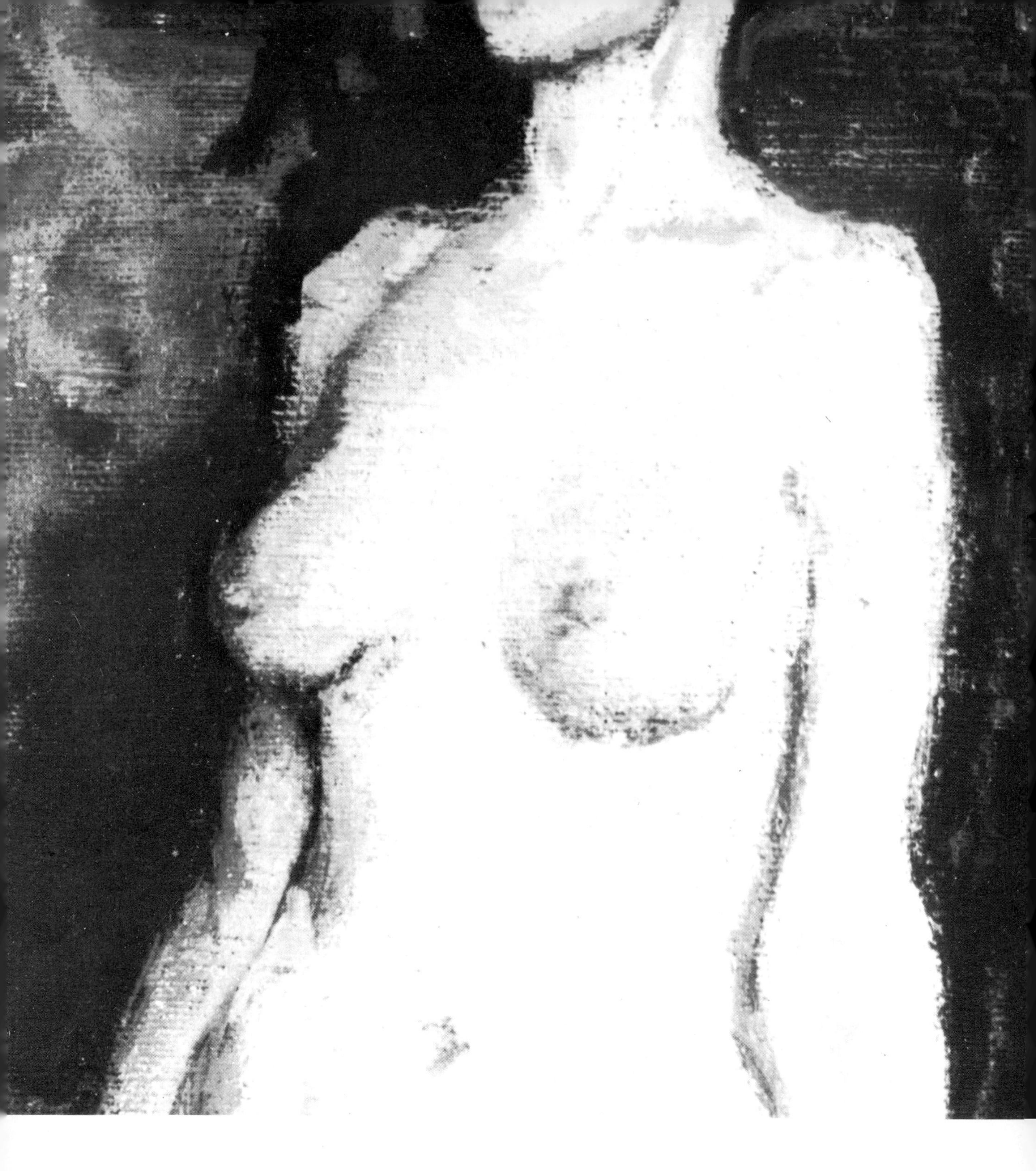

*Detail of torso, final stage.*

*Detail of legs, final stage.*

*Detail of hand, final stage.*

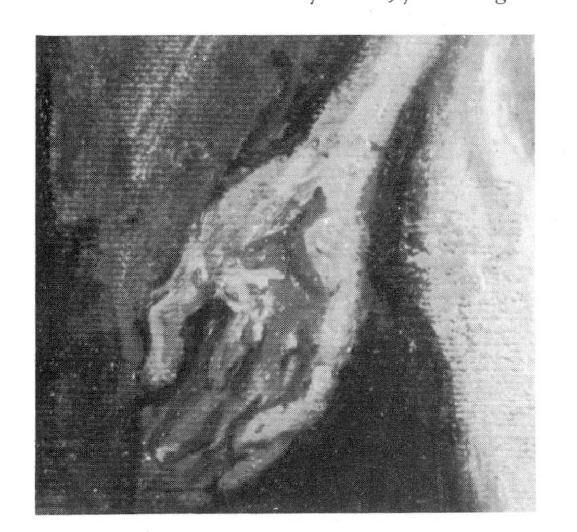

*Detail of hand, final stage.*

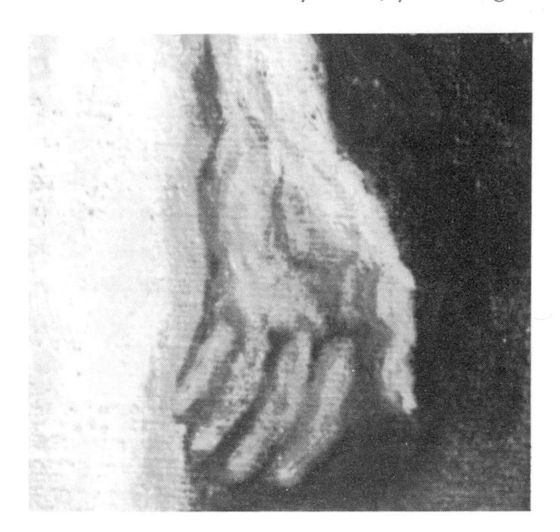

# 7 THE RECLINING FIGURE

THE reclining figure offers problems in distribution of weight, foreshortening, and disposition on the picture surface, to a greater extent than the standing figure.

By the distribution of weight, I mean manipulating the line and the light and shade so that the parts of the figure lying on the couch are indeed resting *on* the couch and not floating above it. Emphasizing the shadow area between the figure and the couch helps weld the two to create the illusion of the body's weight on an object.

In foreshortening (perspective applied to a single object), begin by freely drawing the entire gesture of the figure. Then return to the part of the figure nearest you—in this case, the head. Draw what you see—not without employing your knowledge of the figure—and the rest will fall easily into place.

The disposition of the figure on the picture surface refers not only to the placement of the figure to the right or left of the canvas, but also to the pattern or design created by the figure and the area *around* the figure.

The reclining nude is one of the classic poses for interpreting the human figure: Venus by Giorgione, Titian, and Velásquez; Rembrandt's



ODALISQUE *Private collection.*

Danae; Goya's Maja; Ingres' Odalisques; Manet's Olympia, to name a few. It is essential that you draw and paint the reclining nude, despite its difficulties, if you wish to understand the human figure in all of its aspects.

The reclining pose I have used here offers contrasts of curved and straight lines that set up a rhythm creating a feeling of movement (in spite of the figure's immobility).

## *First stage*

First, note how the figure is placed on the canvas: the bulk of the figure is lying well within the rectangle, occupying most of the picture surface. Although the figure is supine, the pose is dynamic with maximum use made of the curves and angles of the body, an element which creates a more interesting and exciting picture.

The figure is very freely drawn with almost no attention given to detail. Rather, my aim was to capture the over-all form and movement, the gesture of the figure. The directions of the pelvis and rib-cage are well established, and the various parts of the figure are reduced to basic shapes.

Although the couch is barely indicated at this stage, it establishes the figure lying *on* something and not just floating in the air.

The areas of light and shadow are brushed in, not only to show the play of light, but also to help define the form.

## *Second stage*

Here I have blocked in the colors. Working from dark to light, I have covered the areas of light and shadow. I keep the darks transparent and use more paint in the lights. Since the source of light is above and to the left of

FIRST STAGE *I placed the figure on the canvas so that the major portion is lying well within the rectangle, occupying most of the picture surface. In spite of the immobility, the post is dynamic rather than static, with a maximum use made of the curves and angles of the body. I drew the figure freely, paying almost no attention to detail.*

*Detail of torso, first stage.*

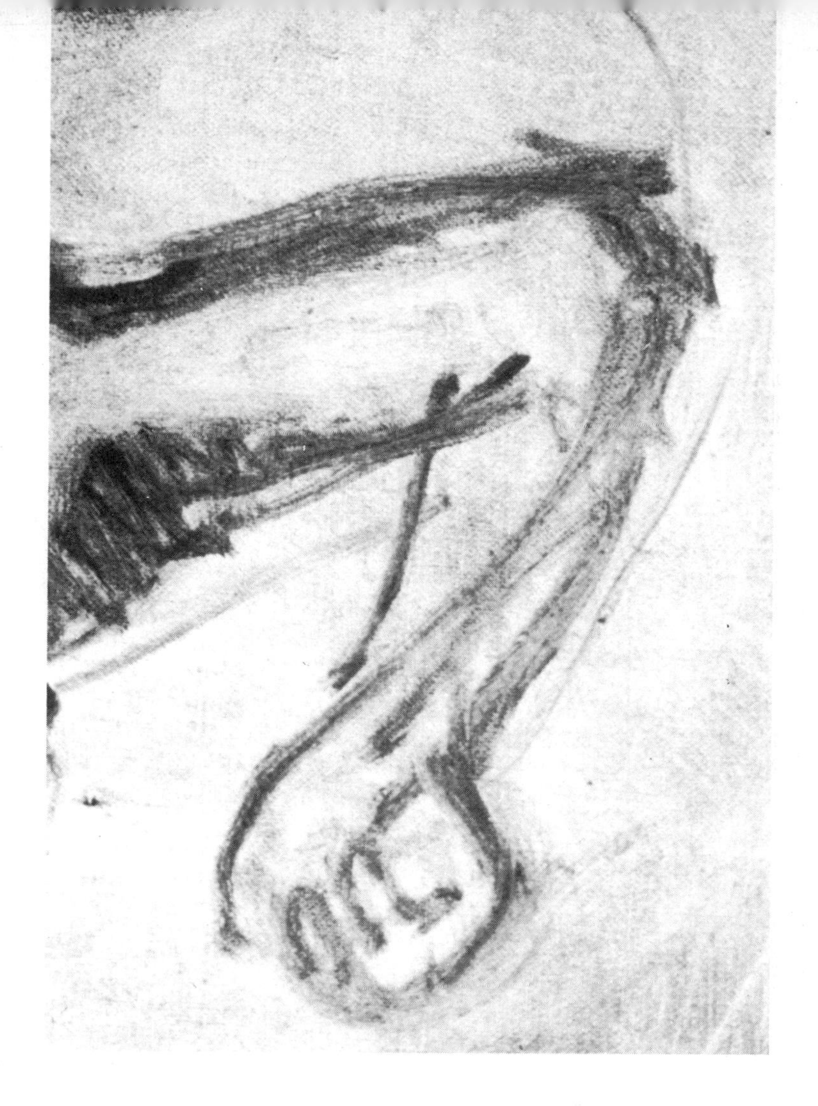

*Detail of arm, first stage.*

the figure, the main areas of shadow naturally fall on the right side of the figure. However, you must not allow the cast shadows to destroy the interior modeling of the figure, and thus lose the form.

I usually use dark contour lines in a rather broken, segmented fashion. Doing this helps to define the form and also maintains the two-dimensional aspect of the painting, while modeling in light and shade creates the illusion of the third dimension.

The painting technique employed is a very personal and individual thing. My approach depends very little on my subject. As with most artists, the way I draw and paint is fundamentally the same for all subjects and compositions, regardless of whether I am painting a reclining or standing figure, a landscape, or a bowl of fruit. The basic problems are always the same: drawing, composition, color, and texture.

*Detail of torso, second stage.*

SECOND STAGE *Using dark contour lines in a rather broken, segmented fashion helps define the form, and also maintains the two-dimensional aspect of the painting. At the same time, modeling in light and shade creates the illusion of the third dimension.*

## *Third stage*

I achieved a satisfying contrast by painting the color of the figure predominately yellow-orange and the surrounding area its complementary color blue.

I have spoken earlier of the way in which warm tones come forward and cool tones recede. You must take this characteristic into account in your painting, and saturate the foreground with orange, yellow, and red, and paint the most distant parts green, violet, and blue.

The artist, working from nature, applies his most violent tones on the lighted parts and, once he has achieved the desired effect, immediately surrounds the light parts with tones of the same value, but inclining to gray. These grays are tinted with blue, proportionately to the amount of orange contained in the lighted parts. Actually, you could say that the colorist's art consists of discreetly distributing grays around the strongly colored parts of the picture.

In this stage of making the picture, my aim is again toward an over-all harmony and unity of the picture's various elements. One of the beginner's main faults is putting a little of everything everywhere, neglecting the idea of the whole. The beginner tends to paint a little color, a little gray, a little contrast, a little light, a little shade. The result is weakness and the painting lacks unity and expression.

THIRD STAGE *Warm tones tend to come forward and cool tones seem to recede. You must take this characteristic into account when you paint. Saturate the foreground with orange, yellow, and red and the most distant parts with green, violet, and blue. In its final form, "Reclining Nude" moves from warm tones in the foreground to a cool blue background. Courtesy, ACA Gallery, New York.*

*Detail of arm, second stage.*

*Detail of arm, final stage.*

*Detail of torso, final stage.*

M.Soyer

# 8 MULTIPLE FIGURE COMPOSITION

IN their book, *A Dictionary of Art and Artists,* Peter and Linda Murray define composition by calling it, "The art of combining the elements of a picture into a satisfactory whole." The authors go on to say, "In art the whole is very much more than the sum of its parts. A picture is well composed if its constituents—whether figures or apples or just shapes —form a harmony which pleases the eye when regarded as two-dimensional shapes on a flat ground. This is the sole aim of most abstract painting, but in more traditional forms [which is what interests us here] the task is made much more difficult by the need to project the forms in an ordered sequence into an imaginary depth or picture space without losing their effectiveness as a pattern."

It is unfortunate that today the beginner attaches only slight importance to the problems of composition and to the things connected with constructing the picture. This is perhaps understandable, undermined as the beginner is by the unprecedented state of chaos and anarchy which exists in all of the arts. He is bombarded on every side by abstract expressionism and abstract impressionism, hard-edged abstraction, pop art, and a host of other highly touted revolutionary *isms* vying for his attention.



SIX DANCERS *Collection, Mr. and Mrs. Joseph Orlan.*

Generally, if the beginner thinks at all about composition, he does so in either emotional or literary terms. For him, composition is a matter of objects or figures describing an action or an emotion. This is viewing the problem from its least important aspect. What is actually important is creating a plastic, self-sufficient whole. The emotion or the anecdote that may have provided the subject matter is merely the point of departure.

So, when attempting a multiple figure composition, such as the one illustrated here, your foremost concern should be with line, form, color, and value. This is not to discount the importance of emotion and idea in art, but merely to emphasize that no matter what the picture "means" or what activity the figures are engaged in (if any) and no matter how lofty the artist's aims may be, it is all meaningless if the composition is weak, the drawing poor, and the color muddy.

## *First stage*

In this composition of seven figures, I used the same model for each pose. Doing this helps produce a homogeneity that would not be possible if seven different models were used, a method that would draw too much attention to the physical differences in the figures. Several models would detract from my aim of complete harmony.

Often I combine figures from several drawings into a composite sketch. After working out a satisfactory composition, I have my model assume the different poses for the actual painting.

Working from my composite sketch, I freely drew in the figures of the composition in umber on my toned canvas. The placement and attitude of each figure is designed to achieve a harmonious whole employing a considerable amount of contrast at the same time. Five figures are standing and two are seated. Four figures are clothed and three are nude. The

FIRST STAGE *Working from a composite sketch on paper, I freely drew the figures of the composition in umber on my toned canvas. The placement and attitude of each figure is designed to achieve a harmonious whole, employing a considerable amount of contrast at the same time.*

*Detail of foreground figure, first stage.*

seated figure in the foreground looks out, while the other figures gaze in various directions.

While the shape of the canvas is square, the character of the composition is predominately vertical. There is a rhythm in the disposition of the figures, starting with the curve of the back of the seated figure in the foreground carrying the eye from one figure to another and back again. Through this flow of curved and straight lines, unity and harmony is achieved in the picture. Also note the repetition of shapes, curves, and

*Detail of foreground figure, second stage.*

angles that build a unified pattern. As I paint, I always consider the painting in its totality.

## *Second stage*

Here I began to establish the darks and lights and to block in the colors. I tried to keep the patterns of color and value simple.

*Detail of foreground figure, final stage.*

As you can see here, the figures and background are all advanced together. I do not treat each figure or a part of a figure separately, or leave the background until last. Instead, I consider the entire picture simultaneously. For example, while painting in the upper left-hand corner. I consider what is necessary in the lower right-hand corner.

SECOND STAGE *As you can see here, the figures and background are all advanced together. I do not treat each figure or a part of a figure separately, or leave the background until last. Instead, I consider the entire picture simultaneously.*

By bringing some of the color of the figures into the background and some of the background colors into the figures, I achieve a tapestry-like unity of color. If the color of an object seems to separate too much from the picture or is discordant, place a piece of colored paper or cloth over the trouble spot. In that way you can determine what color seems right.

## *Third stage*

Avoid too much "finish" in the picture. By finishing some parts and leaving other parts less finished, you direct the eye to the main points of interest in the picture, and you also create another source of contrast.

As I painted, I continued to improve the drawing, keeping in mind the whole—the over-all movement. All parts of the picture must work toward the expression of this end. Features or clothing or accessories must all be treated as factors in the general movement. However interesting these details may be in themselves, in a painting they are parts of a sequence. This unity is more important than individual details. Throughout the whole canvas you must also think of the effect of big masses of color relating to each other.

Notice that even the brush strokes have a rhythmical relation to one another. Also notice how the strokes in the background follow the contour of the figures, a technique which helps mold the picture into a whole.

THIRD STAGE *As I painted, I continued to improve the drawing, keeping in mind the over-all movement. All parts of the picture must work toward the expression of this end. Features or clothing or accessories must all be treated as specific factors in the general movement. "Seven Dancers" is in the collection of Mrs. Ida Soyer.*

*Detail of background figures, final stage.*

*Detail of background figures, final stage.*

# 9 TRAINING THE PROFESSIONAL ARTIST

HOW does one become an artist? Can art be learned? After teaching for many years, I still do not know how to answer these questions. However, I can tell you how art has been taught during several periods in history.

## *Renaissance apprenticeships*

In the time of the Renaissance, a father would apprentice his talented boy to a professional painter, a *master* of painting. The young boy would first be taught how to grind colors; how to prepare canvas and walls for fresco painting; and how to trace cartoons (large preliminary drawings) on canvases and walls.

Later, when the apprentice showed ability, the master would allow him to paint one of the figures in the background. Or the young artist would be allowed to execute a piece of drapery in one of the master's paintings.

When the young boy approached maturity in his art and became pro-



PORTRAIT OF THE ARTIST WITH SKETCHBOOK *Collection, Mr. and Mrs. Herbert A. Goldstone.*

ficient, the master would begin to rely on him and allow him to do more important things. So it was with the beautiful "Annunciation" by Verrocchio in the Uffizi Gallery. Verrocchio was the teacher of Leonardo da Vinci. In that picture, so the story goes, the master allowed young Leonardo to design and paint the now famous figure of the angel.

Artists developed in this manner, became masters in their turn, and had pupils apprenticed to them.

## *The academies*

A later development in art education was the academy. The academy of the Carracci brothers in Bologna was the prototype of such schools.

In these schools, students were taught how to work, first from antique casts and then from life. The model was simply set in front of the students and they drew and painted. The instructor came around once or twice a week to criticize their work and correct their mistakes. Otherwise, the student was left on his own.

Since the ambitious young artist often did more work outside the school than in it, he was less constantly and intimately supervised by his teacher than was the Renaissance apprentice by *his* master. Yet even this kind of schooling, like that of the Renaissance, gave the student a sense of security. It gave him training and, above all, discipline. He had to learn to draw and paint before becoming an artist on his own.

## *Today's art boom*

While these schools and academies still exist, they have changed. With today's "art explosion," the "anybody can paint" philosophy, and the "art

SEATED DANCER *This is a study of a young dancer with legs spread, dressed in a black leotard and a long red-orange skirt. The wall is dark brown. It is a small painting, but since the figure takes up almost the entire canvas, the painting seems much larger. Private collection.*

as therapy" movement, the schools now admit not only the serious art student, but also the amateur, the prematurely retired "golden ager," the bored suburban housewife, the mentally ill in need of treatment, and others for whom art is a pleasant and rewarding pastime. From the social point of view, this is a good thing. It also helps, perhaps, to create a knowledgeable audience for art. But such training has little to do with the making of a professional artist.

Art education has now been taken over by colleges and universities. This is especially true in the United States. Today, a young man or woman can go to college and "major" in art. Along with philosophy, languages, mathematics, and science, he will have several hours each week of art appreciation, art history, theory of design, printmaking, fabric design, advertising layout, painting, and welding (so much in style today). The result is a well rounded jack-of-all-trades, perhaps a Master of Arts, but *not* an artist.

The very nature of college education is segmentation. The college art student rushes from three hours of Drawing 101 to his next course in Clay Modeling 203, perhaps. At the end of the semester, he is supposedly ready for Drawing 102. But does this make him a draftsman? I think not.

Art is complete immersion. One does not stop drawing or painting at the sound of a bell and rush to the next class. A serious art student may work seven hours at one problem, without interruption, and then continue in the evening. A college program does not allow for this sustained, single-minded labor.

These students are not told that they must learn to draw the human figure in proportion and foreshortening. They are immediately encouraged to "experiment" and to "express themselves," both favorite phrases today. In the end, these young people lack the feeling of security in their knowledge and ability, a security that the students of the Renaissance and the students of the academy did have. Today's students are left to themselves.

IDA AND MARTHA *This portrait of my wife and her little dog, Martha, is somewhat unusual in color: lavender, blues, and red-violet. The figure and high-backed chair are silhouetted against the light background. Collection, Mr. and Mrs. Percy Uris.*

M. Soyer

They are not given a sense of basic values. They have no one to tell them, in their formative years, what is good and what is bad.

And so the students are graduated with bachelors degrees, masters degrees, and doctoral degrees in art. They, in turn, get jobs in colleges teaching students by the same doubtful method. Thus, more Bachelors and Masters of Arts are created, but, I am afraid, no artists.

Let me make it clear that I am not against college education in art. We need art historians, theoreticians, critics, teachers, and curators. But I am writing here about the practitioner of art: the painter, the sculptor, the printmaker, the draftsman. Can you imagine anything more ludicrous than Rembrandt with a PhD?

## *Inspired teaching*

Although I have questioned and criticized the various methods of teaching art today, I do believe that there are inspiring teachers. Fortunate indeed is the student who is touched by such a man at the beginning of his career.

I shall never forget meeting Robert Henri. At that time, I was a student at the National Academy of Design. My teachers were drab and unimaginative. They insisted on correct proportion, via the plumb line, and belated impressionistic technique in painting. Henri taught in a small school in Spanish Harlem. A friend of mine took me there. The moment I saw Henri, I knew I wanted to be like him.

Henri was an artist and I wanted to be an artist too. He was alive, electric, so different from the stultified teachers at the Academy. He would not criticize the so-called correctness of a drawing, but rather the student's point of view. He talked about the philosophy of art and the esthetics of art.

STUDIO INTERIOR WITH TWO FIGURES *This is a large painting in which I tried to express the contrast of youth and age. The colors are predominately blues, purples, and grays. The paint is comparatively thin and uniform throughout. Courtesy, ACA Gallery, New York.*

He used what seemed to me, at that time, somewhat abstract terms. For instance, he would say: "This line does not function." Or "The form is weak." About the composition, he might say: "It begins from nowhere and ends nowhere." He would say: "Your color lacks vibrancy." He would harshly criticize mere cleverness or the desire to astonish.

Henri would often refer us to Rembrandt, Manet, or other artists, thus making us haunt the museums. He taught at art schools all his life, producing such artists as Bellows, Sloan, and Hopper; yet he would talk against schools and their rigid methods. A rebel himself, he inspired and encouraged rebellion in his students.

What, then, does this all come down to? What is good art education? I can only answer from my own life.

I believe in discipline and I believe in freedom. It may not be easy to combine the two; but if you study the mature paintings of great artists, you will find that they contain both discipline and freedom.

I believe in constant, steady work. I am against waiting for inspiration (one may wait in vain). I draw two mornings a week. I paint every day. Even when a day's results are disappointing, the day has not been lost. It has been spent in the practice of painting. I do not believe in teaching the technique of painting as a set of fixed procedures. Technique is the artist's personal language, setting him apart from other artists. This language will evolve in time.

I hope I have not been too platitudinous in this book; but, then, a truth often repeated can begin to sound like a platitude precisely because it is so true.

I believe that the human being is the noblest creation on earth and that the theme of man—man at work, man in his landscape, man at play—is therefore the noblest theme in art.

An artist should not only be judged by his technique, but by his versa-

STUDIO INTERIOR WITH TWO MEN *This is a self-portrait with my dog in my lap and a friend in the background. The whole painting is in greenish-grays with touches of red and purple in my suit and in the pictures on the wall. Private collection.*

tility, by his findings. He should also be judged by his philosophy, by his theme, by his point of view.

To me, the greatest paintings of Cézanne are not his landscapes and still lifes—beautiful though they are—but rather his card players, his portraits of men and women, his peasants, bathers, and his psychologically revealing self-portraits. Winslow Homer's advice to a young artist, whom he observed one day painting a rocky Maine landscape was: "Paint Man. Leave the rocks to old artists like me."

I believe that art should mirror life, that an artist should always study, search and question. He should not be satisfied with his successes. He should, in the words of Thomas Mann, "wear, so to say, [his] eyebrows permanently lifted."

# INDEX